AF539295

Panza

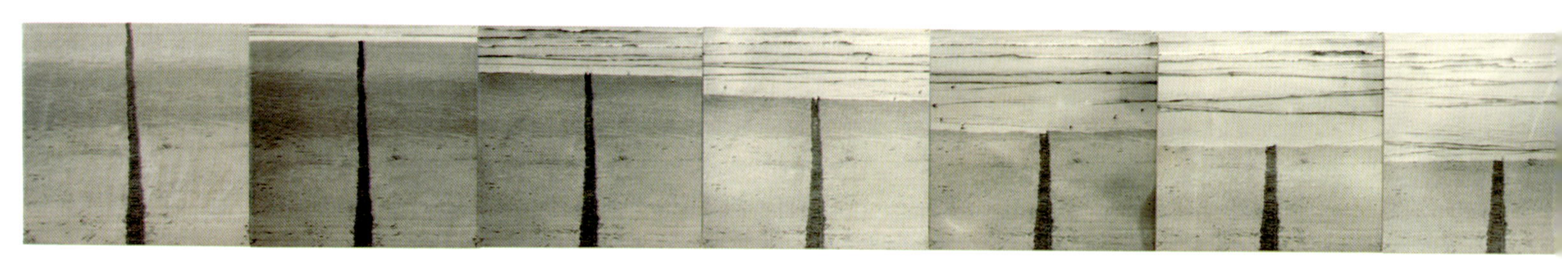

The Panza Collection

Evelyn C. Hankins

Giuseppe Panza

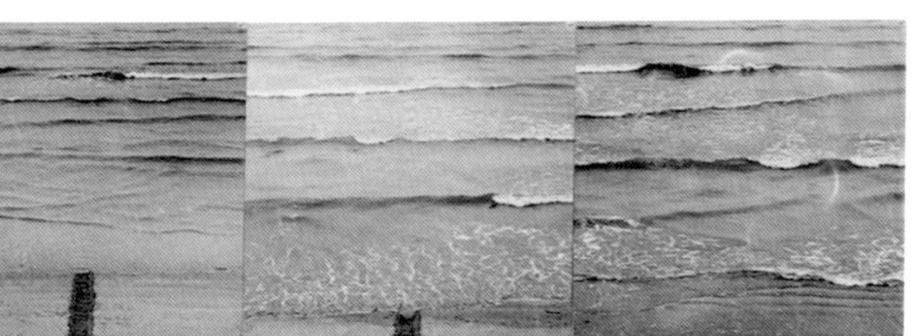

Panza

Hirshhorn Museum and Sculpture Garden

This catalogue is published in conjunction with the exhibition *The Panza Collection*, organized by the Hirshhorn Museum and Sculpture Garden, Smithsonian Institution, Washington, DC.

Hirshhorn Museum and Sculpture Garden, Washington, DC
October 23, 2008–
January 11, 2009

The exhibition is made possible by the Holenia Trust in memory of Joseph H. Hirshhorn, the Friends of Jim and Barbara Demetrion Endowment Fund, and the Hirshhorn's Board of Trustees with additional support from the Museum's National Benefactors.

Edited by Deborah E. Horowitz, Hirshhorn Museum and Sculpture Garden

Designed by Hal Kugeler Ltd.

Printed by Lowitz + Sons, Chicago

© 2008 the authors and Hirshhorn Museum and Sculpture Garden, Smithsonian Institution, Washington, DC

All rights reserved. No part of this publication may be reproduced or transmitted in any form or by any means, electronic or mechanical, including photocopy, recording, or any other information storage and retrieval system, without prior permission in writing from the Hirshhorn Museum and Sculpture Garden, Smithsonian Institution, Washington, DC.

ISBN 978-0-9789063-1-3

Hirshhorn Museum
and Sculpture Garden
Smithsonian Institution
Independence Avenue at
Seventh Street, SW
MRC 353 PO Box 37012
Washington, DC 20013-7012
www.hirshhorn.si.edu

Available through D.A.P./
Distributed Art Publishers
155 Sixth Avenue, 2nd Floor
New York, NY 10013
Tel: (212) 627-1999
Fax: (212) 627-9484

COVER
Robert Barry
American, b. New York, New York, 1936
Steel Disc Suspended ⅛ in. Above Floor, 1967
Steel and nylon string
Dimensions variable;
disc 2 inches diameter × ⅝ inches high
Joseph H. Hirshhorn Purchase Fund, 2007
The Panza Collection (07.36)

FRONTISPIECE
Jan Dibbets
Dutch, b. Weert, The Netherlands, 1941
Flood Tide, 1969
Gelatin silver prints
Overall 23¾ × 237⅛ inches
Joseph H. Hirshhorn Purchase Fund, 2007
The Panza Collection (07.43)

hirshhorn

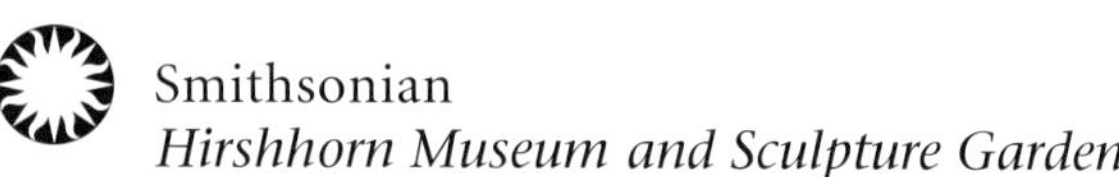

Contents

7 **Foreword**
Kerry Brougher

11 **The Panza Collection at the Hirshhorn**
Giuseppe Panza

15 **Collecting the Uncollectible**
Evelyn C. Hankins

29 **Plates**

96 **Photography Credits**

Foreword

Roman Opalka
Polish, b. Abbeville, France, 1931
Detail of *1965/1–∞: Detail 460260–484052*, Begun 1965
Acrylic paint on canvas
77 × 53¼ inches
Joseph H. Hirshhorn Purchase Fund, 2007
The Panza Collection (07.71)

A collection built by the dedication and enthusiasm for art of one man. This statement equally characterizes the remarkable array of artworks gathered by the Hirshhorn Museum and Sculpture Garden's founder, Joseph H. Hirshhorn, and Count Giuseppe Panza di Biumo. Although distinct in their interests, both men early in their collecting careers resolved to concentrate on the art of their time. Both took a focused approach, being more intent on acquiring specific artists' work in depth than in amassing a vast range of pieces. Both became committed to placing their collections in public institutions in order to ensure that they would be accessible to a broad audience.

Beginning in 1956, Dr. Panza began to create one of the great collections of American and European contemporary art, primarily in the areas of Abstract Expressionist, Pop, Minimal, and Conceptual art of the 1950s, 1960s, and 1970s. Rather than purchase the complete spectrum of an artist's oeuvre, he instead concentrated his efforts on purchasing numerous pieces from the best period of artists' output and often very early in their careers. His abiding interest in the philosophy and ideas behind each work of art also guided his pioneering approach and led him to acquire not only painting and sculpture, but also Environmental and Light and Space art—distinguishing him from most collectors of his time.

Over the last two decades, Dr. Panza has sold and donated significant portions of his collection to a small, select number of American museums, primarily The Museum of Contemporary Art, Los Angeles and the Guggenheim Museum. As he has always prioritized maintaining bodies of work from his collection over selling works individually, in both of these instances pieces were kept together that created coherent groupings; at MOCA, the focus was on Abstract Expressionism and Pop Art, while Minimal and Conceptual art were at the core of the Guggenheim's acquisition.

It was during his tenure as board member at the Museum of Contemporary Art, Los Angeles, in the early 1980s, that I first met Dr. Panza. As curator, I had the privilege of collaborating with him on an exhibition of his works as well as the acquisition and accompanying catalogue. I was impressed then by his attention to detail, his aesthetic sensibility, and his knowledge and enthusiasm for the artworks he had amassed over the years.

My association with him continued when I became Chief Curator at the Hirshhorn, and after many thoughtful meetings and discussions about the pieces in his collection, the Museum was able to purchase a group of works that substantially enhance its holdings of Conceptual, Minimal, Light and Space, and Environmental art.

In total, thirty-nine pieces by sixteen artists have been added to the collection. Not only do these works fill the Conceptual Art gap in the Museum's holdings, but, in many cases, they also round out holdings by specific artists, and in nine instances are the first acquired by these significant artists. Many of the selections have been made with the intention of creating room-sized installations that best showcase each artist. In other cases, they were chosen because each augments the holdings of artists already in the collection.

The opening of *The Panza Collection* and the publication of this catalogue mark the culmination of this fruitful collaboration, and the Museum is pleased to present these impressive works to the public for the first time. In addition, we are grateful that Dr. Panza and his wife Giovanna agreed to explore the Hirshhorn's nearly 12,000 objects and create an installation as part of our *Ways of Seeing* series to accompany the exhibition, providing further insight into the vision of this renowned collector.

In addition to Giuseppe and Giovanna Panza, I would like to extend my thanks to their daughter Giuseppina and son Alessandro for all of their assistance with this project. Their graciousness with their time and expertise has been an invaluable asset. Thanks are also due to all of the artists, their studios, and estates as well as their galleries for all of their cooperation and input. I would also like to thank Roland Lusk, Lacey Fekishazy, and John Hogan for their meticulous skill in executing the Sol LeWitt wall drawing.

I am grateful to the entire Hirshhorn staff for their efforts to make the acquisition, exhibition, and publication of this important collection possible. First and foremost, thanks to associate curator Evelyn Hankins for working closely with Dr. Panza and his wife on all aspects of the exhibition as well as their *Ways of Seeing* installation and for her excellent contribution to this catalogue. Thanks also to managing editor Deborah Horowitz and publications assistant Caitlin Woolsey for editing and producing the catalogue, the design of which is the result of the thoughtful vision of Hal Kugeler.

Although it is not possible to include all staff members by name here, I do want to acknowledge former director Olga Viso for her support of this acquisition; curator Anne Ellegood and director of collections management Susan Lake for their assistance and keen eye during the selection process. I am also grateful to Al Masino, Beth Skirkanich, John Klink, Scott Larson, and the entire exhibits staff for their inventiveness and problem-solving abilities; photographer Lee Stalsworth for ensuring that all of the images are reproduced at the highest standards; Barbara Freund and Keri Towler for their deft handling of registrarial issues; Emily Shaw and Bob Allen for their creative designs for exhibition materials; Milena Kalinovska, Ryan Hill, Kevin Hull, and everyone in the programs department for planning all of the associated events, lectures, and talks; Roni Polisar, Jeff Martin, Clarke Bedford, and the entire conservation staff for ensuring the condition of the works; Gabriel Riera, Vanessa Mallory, Jennifer Rossi, and Erin Baysden for their work to market the exhibition; Kevin Crysler, Jennifer Barrett, and the entire development team for their fundraising efforts; Al Miner and Karen Perry for their assistance throughout the project with logistical arrangements; José Ortiz, Rich Reichley, and April Martin as well as exhibition coordinator Lawrence Hyman for overseeing all administrative, budget, and contract details. Special thanks are also due to interns Karin Casper, Anne Shires, and Rachel White for their assistance.

I would also like to express my gratitude to our Board of Trustees, especially our chairman Tom Hill and our former vice chair Mitch Rales, for their support of this acquisition and exhibition. Thanks are also due to the Holenia Trust in memory of Joseph H. Hirshhorn, the Friends of Jim and Barbara Demetrion Endowment Fund, and the Museum's National Benefactors for their support.

Kerry Brougher
Acting Director and Chief Curator
Hirshhorn Museum
and Sculpture Garden

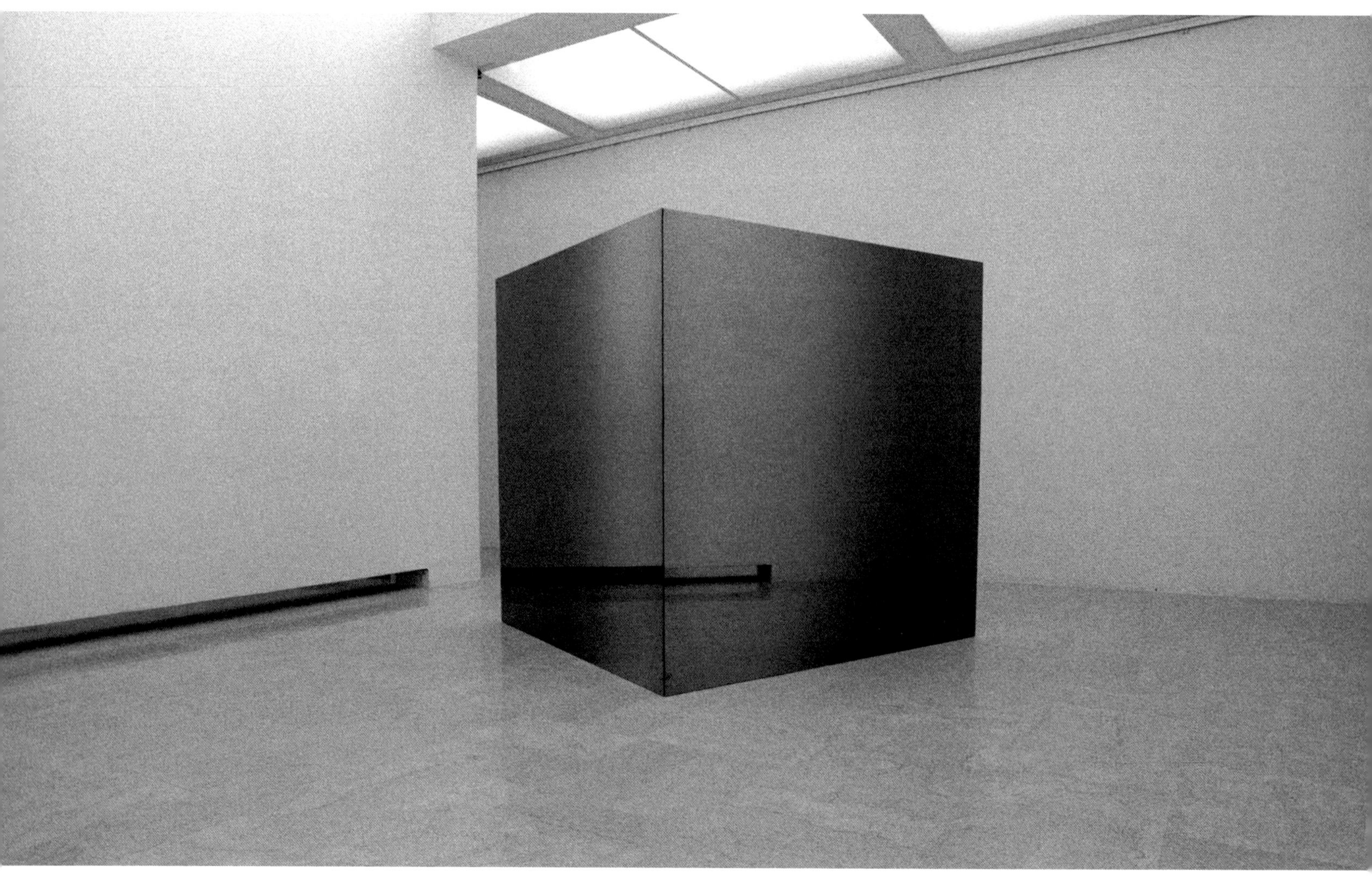

Larry Bell
American, b. Chicago, Illinois, 1939
Untitled, 1973
Vacuum-plated glass
Each panel 72 × 72 × ⅜ inches
Joseph H. Hirshhorn Purchase Fund, 2007
The Panza Collection (07.40)

The Panza Collection at the Hirshhorn

Giuseppe Panza

I have always been absorbed by ancient and modern art and also have an interest in philosophy. I consider the best art to offer an opportunity for contemplation. Initial impressions are our first link to a work, but, in order to have a complete understanding of its quality, it is necessary to appreciate its underlying rationale.

Behind every great work of art lay ideas, and through ideas you can determine a philosophy. In each historical age there are dominant ideas and philosophies, but also those that will not be intimidated by the more prevailing ones. To discover just what these ideas and philosophies are leads to a complete understanding of the beauty of a work of art. I began to collect American art in the 1950s with works by Franz Kline, Mark Rothko, and Robert Rauschenberg, all artists completely different from each other. Each represented ideas and feelings of various kinds.

For Kline, it was a question of vital energy that exploded as he attempted to reach the highest, perhaps unobtainable, aims paired with his awareness of the very impossibility of attaining these goals and of their withdrawal, perhaps even their demise. His paintings, black marks on white canvas, efficiently convey the sadness of hopes too great to become reality—a romantic attitude.

Rothko was in search of eternal happiness, quite beyond anything that might be discovered by contemplation or an examination of ourselves: he believed colors could express all the emotions within us.

In Rauschenberg, I saw the recovery of the past through objects used and abandoned every day. Life consumed by time but experienced once more in the mind. It was a meditation on the inexorable flow of things that change and die.

In 1962, Pop Art was born. The threat of the bomb had diminished, industrial production had grown, and goods were available to all. A new age of well-being had begun. Imagery from advertising and popular literature testified to this change. Such artists as Lichtenstein, Oldenburg, and Rosenquist interpreted this victory of consumerism as the occasion for reflecting on the difference between appearance and reality.

Almost at the same time, in 1963, a completely distinct train of thought was developing: Minimalism. A search for what is essential. It was necessary to eliminate everything superfluous in order to arrive at the truth. It was an extremely rigorous commitment that immediately revealed any errors. Only the most intellectually strong came out victorious; the weakest, those who did not know how to discern the rationale behind objective reality, were eliminated. Euclidian geometry became the expressive means. The rigors of logic dictated the variety of forms. Humanity's greatest power, thought, was shown it its full beauty.

Minimalism was also the necessary premise for the development of Conceptualism. Particularly at this moment in the history of art, philosophies could be embodied by images. This possibility was realized through the study of language. We make use of sounds, signs, and images to express our will, thoughts, and emotions and to understand those of others. This is a basic condition for living and for constructing a society, but how can all of this exist in a society only through one means: WORDS, whether written or spoken? We are so accustomed to using them that we forget their enormous power. Without words, we would live like insects. Given that language is as much an intuitive as a logical activity, a word can have a range of meanings that change according to the context of what is being said. Because of this diversity, when a word stands by itself, it becomes ambiguous and can express numerous things. This ambiguity can be very interesting for an artist and can generate various thoughts as well as lead to the exploration of one meaning among the many possibilities—a basic need for a real understanding of any work of art. This is the essence of Conceptual Art, and one fundamental to existence. It is not a difficult or overly intellectual art; it is our everyday life. We think when we look at images or hear words. We are HOMO SAPIENS only because we have mysteriously acquired the use of language.

Conceptual Art began between 1965 and 1968, and its main practitioners were Joseph Kosuth, Lawrence Weiner, Robert Barry, and Douglas Huebler. During this period, a similar yet distinct approach was evolving around the world: in Europe, Hanne Darboven preferred to use numbers rather than words as her method of expression; in Britain, Richard Long and Hamish Fulton developed the means to communicate their relationship with nature; in Los Angeles, a different path came about, because Conceptualism's forms were basically determined by intellectual activity. Los Angeles' Environmental Art was founded on three fundamental elements: space, light, and introspection. Space equals freedom, allowing us to move without limits. Light is another indispensable need. When it is absent, we can know nothing; we remain imprisoned in our own mind and are unable to escape our own consciousness. Only our heartbeat is certain. We become blind—the greatest disability of all. Thought is the highest of human activities, and beyond it there is only ecstatic rapture within infinity, something experienced by few, perhaps only for a moment. But such contemplation is allowed to poor mortals like us though it needs great willpower. For this reason, this level of thought and awareness is not widely undertaken, but is in the UNIVERSE because it enables us to say "I AM." Stars exist but do not know they do so. This is the moment of truth, when we examine ourselves, our will, our aims, our desires. When we can immerse ourselves in our consciousness and discover with pleasure its immense beauty. This is what Robert Irwin's and Doug Wheeler's rooms are about: making possible such a private and individual experience.

The years 1950–75 were among the most creative of the twentieth century, as were the years 1905–29. In these two periods, there was an almost unparalleled evolution in Western and world culture. But after 1975, with the assertion of post modernism, the values that had spurred this evolution were rejected. The gulf between high and low art has widened. Now contemporary art is often confused with art merchandise, something produced in order to be appreciated and bought by those who are not looking for the ideas that make real art possible and permanent.

The art of the last quarter of the twentieth century produced artistic personalities no less important than those of the earlier period, but they have been marginalized because their work is less commercial than that of the present. In forty years' time, when further histories of this crucial period are written, many names that are famous today will disappear and others, now ignored, will have a second life.

The Hirshhorn Museum is located in the cultural center of the nation's capital and is part of the Smithsonian Institution. In the past, the Hirshhorn has had directors like Ned Rifkin and James Demetrion who substantially improved the collection with important acquisitions.

In the last few years, one of my main goals has been to find a museum to acquire many of my works of Conceptual Art, and during a meeting with Kerry Brougher, the Museum's Acting Director and Chief Curator, I realized that the Hirshhorn had the desire to increase its collection in this area. I met Kerry many years ago, when he was a curator at the Museum of Contemporary Art, Los Angeles. I have great esteem for the job he did when we worked together on an exhibition of my collection and for the job he is doing at the Hirshhorn.

After forty years, the interest in Conceptual Art is finally increasing, and there is recognition of what an important achievement of American culture in the 1960s and 1970s it is. The Hirshhorn was given the opportunity to select some of my more interesting Conceptual pieces, and I'm happy that this group of our works, of which I am deeply fond, is now a permanent addition to the Museum's collection.

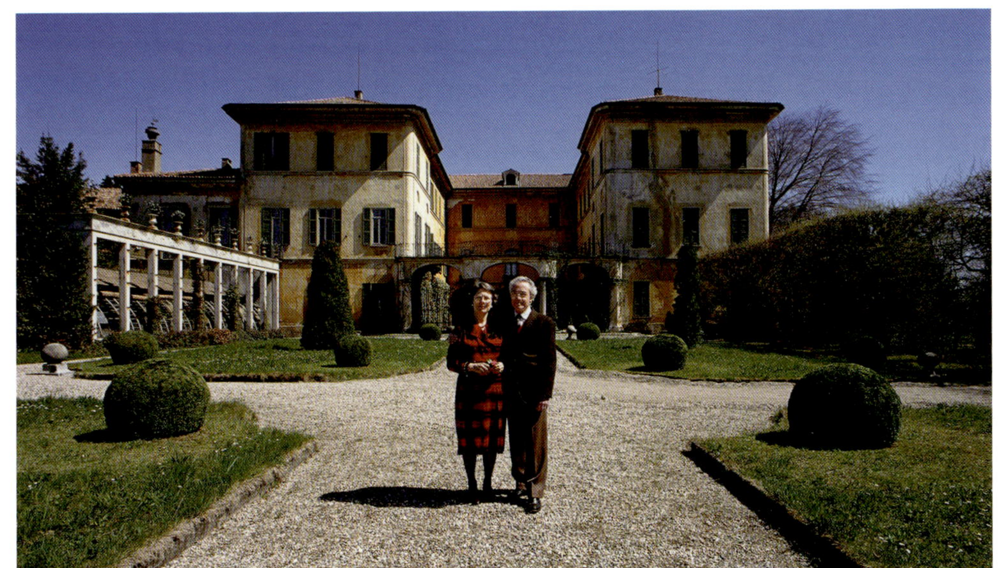

Dr. Giuseppe and Mrs. Giovanna Panza in the grounds at Villa Menafoglio Litta Panza, Varese, Italy

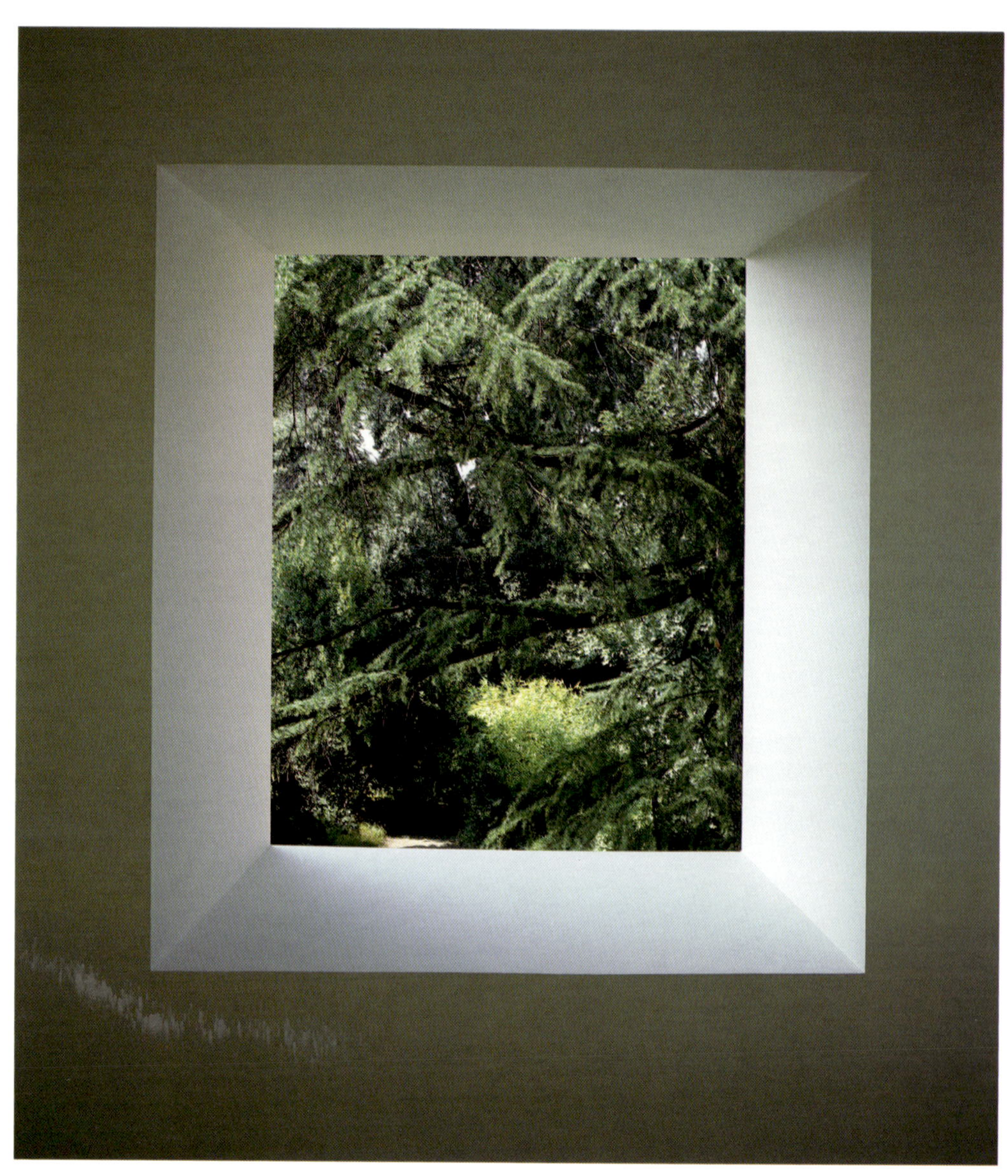

Collecting the Uncollectible

Evelyn C. Hankins

Every passion borders on the chaotic, but the collector's passion borders on the chaos of memories. . . . For what else is this collection but a disorder to which habit has accommodated itself to such an extent that it can appear as order? —Walter Benjamin, 1931

Being an artist now means to question the nature of art. If one is questioning the nature of painting, one cannot be questioning the nature of art. If an artist accepts painting (or sculpture) he is accepting the tradition that goes with it. —Joseph Kosuth, 1969[1]

Robert Irwin
American, b. Long Beach, California, 1928
Varese Portal Room, 1973
Vertical portal cut into exterior wall
The Solomon R. Guggenheim Foundation, New York – Panza Collection, Gift 1992, permanent loan to FAI, Fondo per l'Ambiente Italiano

Villa Menafoglio Litta Panza is an eighteenth-century Italianate and neoclassical manor surrounded by beautifully manicured gardens that overlook the city of Varese, Italy, about thirty minutes north of Milan. In the former service quarters on the second floor, there is a long, white, barrel-vaulted corridor that is broken by a series of open doorways on either side. Ethereal light colored yellow, blue, red, and pink radiates across the thresholds, at once highlighting the surprisingly unembellished beauty of the interior architecture and enticing visitors to experience the solitary, neon light installation by Dan Flavin that is situated in each gallery.[2] The last doorway on the left opens onto a small antechamber followed by a modestly scaled room, which is empty save for a large rectangular aperture that pierces the building's deep exterior wall. Devoid of both ornament and glass, the open portal frames a striking view, which defies expectations by focusing attention on the abstract patterns created by the tree branches directly adjacent to the villa rather than offering a more conventional, sweeping vista of the gardens and surrounding landscape.

The aperture is, in fact, a site-specific artwork by Robert Irwin, commissioned by the villa's owner, Giuseppe Panza di Biumo. Indeed, Irwin's *Varese Portal Room*, 1973, shares certain attributes with Dr. Panza: visionary yet focused, conceptual yet rooted in the sensual, contemporary yet firmly grounded in history. *Varese Portal Room*, moreover, is only one of more than 2,500 artworks in the Panza Collection.[3] Possessing the curiosity and relentless urge to acquire that is singular to collectors (celebrated or not), Dr. Panza has amassed a collection of American and European art that reflects his passion for the avant-garde movements of the second half of the twentieth century. *Varese Portal Room*, though, signals the trait that distinguishes Dr. Panza from other collectors: the drive to acquire hundreds of artworks at exactly the moment when contemporary artists were producing ever more uncollectible works of art. For, in the 1960s, artists in the United States and Europe increasingly resisted the time-honored categories of painting and sculpture and, instead, defined art in a much broader manner, from Conceptual works that favored

Dan Flavin
American, b. Jamaica, New York, 1933–1996
Varese Corridor, 1976
Fluorescent tubing
The Solomon R. Guggenheim Foundation, New York – Panza Collection, Gift 1992, permanent loan to FAI, Fondo per l'Ambiente Italiano

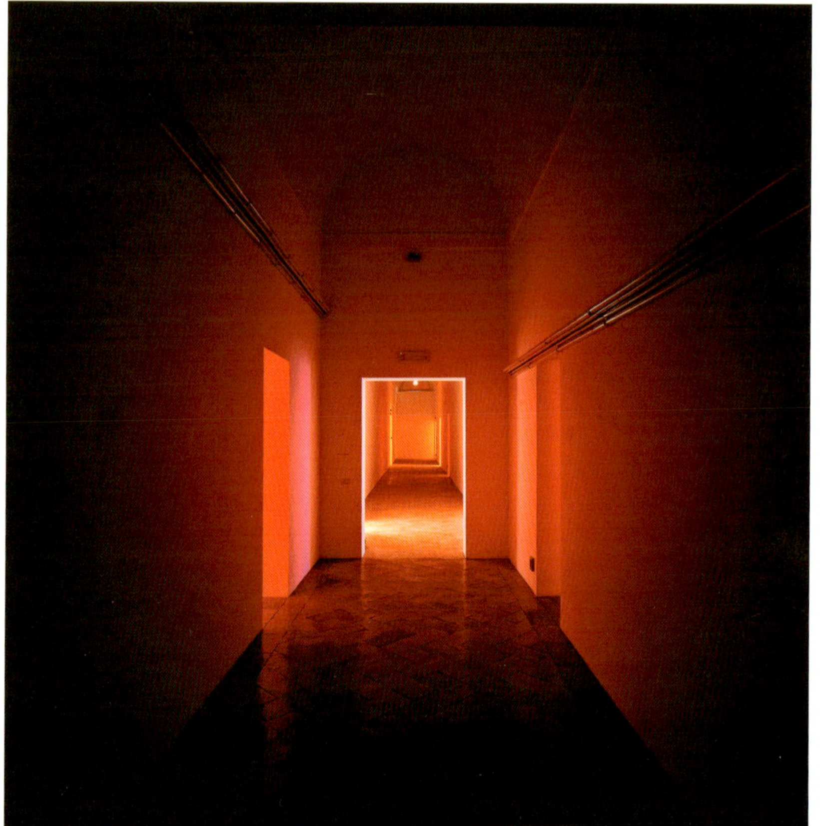

ideas over the creation of unique objects to large-scale installations that challenged existing notions about perception and the boundary between an artwork and the surrounding architecture or environment.

Redefining the Art Object

Giuseppe Panza began to collect contemporary American and European art in 1956 with the purchase of several paintings by Antonio Tàpies from a Paris gallery. The following year, he made what was at that time a radical acquisition: an abstract painting by Franz Kline, which he purchased from Sidney Janis Gallery in New York. Acquired after Dr. Panza had seen the work only in reproduction, Kline's *Buttress,* 1956, cemented what would become a lifelong engagement with contemporary art, particularly works by American artists.[4] Over the next six years, Dr. Panza purchased more than eighty major works by such artists as Robert Rauschenberg, Mark Rothko, Claes Oldenburg, James Rosenquist, and Roy Lichtenstein, thereby establishing himself among the most important and daring collectors of contemporary art.

The works acquired by the Hirshhorn Museum and Sculpture Garden draw from the second phase of Dr. Panza's collecting trajectory. Between 1966 and 1976, he focused on Minimal, Conceptual, Light and Space, and Environmental art, assembling a collection of more than five hundred works by artists ranging from Joseph Kosuth and Sol LeWitt to Robert Irwin and Bruce Nauman. From the outset, Dr. Panza was drawn to artworks characterized by, in his words, "a potent austerity," that "say a lot with a few gestures, eliminating all decoration and unnecessary incidentals."[5] Still, the move from Abstract Expressionism and Pop Art to Minimalism and Conceptual Art encompassed a radical shift in style, media, and, most notably, the notion of what comprises a work of art.

Broadly speaking, the 1960s witnessed a proliferation of innovative approaches to art-making that directly questioned the tenets of Modernism. In particular, artists disputed the relevance of critic Clement Greenberg's formalist ideology, which had monopolized the discourse for almost a decade. Greenberg's absolutist definition of avant-garde art championed work that articulated what was "unique and irreducible" about a specific

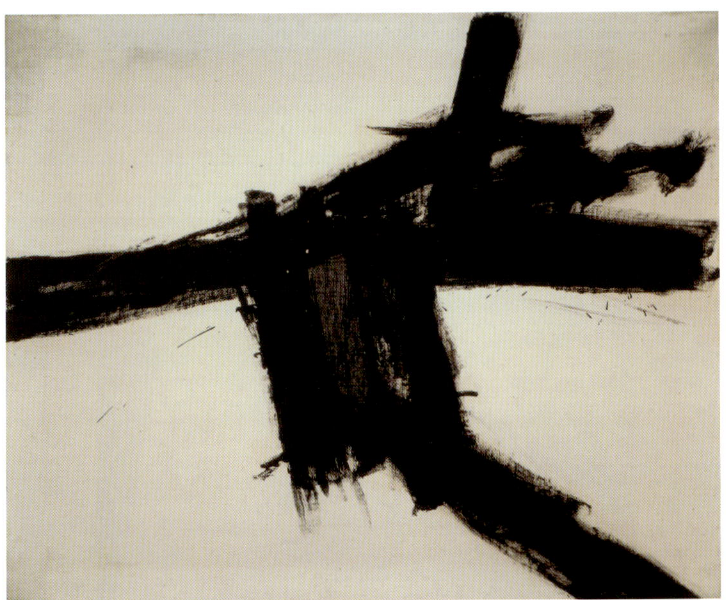

Franz Kline
American, b. Wilkes-Barre, Pennsylvania, 1910–1962
Buttress, 1956
Oil on canvas
46½ x 55½ inches
The Museum of Contemporary Art, Los Angeles
The Panza Collection (86.9)

medium—flatness, in the case of painting—to the exclusion of all other elements, including narrative, figuration, and decoration.[6] Art, according to Greenberg, was essentially optical, to be perceived by the eye alone. And the artists who best epitomized the critic's formalist doctrine, such as Jackson Pollock, Kenneth Noland, and Frank Stella, were upheld by the influential writer as the bellwethers of a seemingly irrefutable canon of Modernism.

The assertion by Pop artists working in the early 1960s that contemporary mass culture offered both viable subjects and techniques launched the first persuasive assault against Greenberg's formalist orthodoxy. Pop Art's abnegation of the artistic subjectivity lauded by Greenberg was reiterated by Minimalism, which refuted the ideas of craftsmanship and the unique aesthetic object through the use of industrial materials and fabrication methods that resulted in uninflected, anonymous surfaces. The Minimalist predilection for reduced, self-referential forms and repetition, importantly, was directed not by purely formal interests, but rather by a new respect for the role that math, logic, and predetermined systems could play in creative practice. Artists such as Donald Judd further subverted both Greenberg's concept of a pure opticality and the conventional artist-object-subject roles by asserting the primacy of phenomenological experience, particularly the ever-shifting relationships between viewer, object, and surrounding space.

Pop Art and Minimalism were just two alternatives that emerged as part of a surge of artistic activity in the mid-1960s. Artists working under the rubrics of Fluxus, Earthworks, Eccentric Abstraction, Performance Art, Conceptual Art, Light and Space Art, and others dramatically expanded the definition of what constituted a work of art. What these diverse approaches shared was their rejection of traditional aesthetic and pictorial concerns, including Greenberg's dogmatic formalism, which was replaced by an avid engagement with ideas, processes, social and political issues, the body, and phenomenological experiences. In short, artists reconsidered the essential nature and meaning of art itself.

Consequently, artists began to create works from an unprecedented array of unorthodox materials, such as text, maps, dirt, video, and light; they also disregarded conventional divisions between the visual and performing arts. Artistic output during this period ranged from ephemeral actions never witnessed by the public to permanent, large-scale installations situated either indoors or out. Much of this work reflected a newly critical stance towards the institutions and social conventions that normally mediated between the artist and public. Artists endeavored to undermine the commodified status of art, for example, by either creating works that could not be sold or disseminating their art via means that circumvented the commercial gallery system. They also cast aside the heroic role of the artist ascribed to preceding generations and instead empowered the public by placing equal emphasis on the creator and viewer in generating meaning.

It was in this context that Dr. Panza resumed his pursuit of contemporary artworks in 1969 after a six-year hiatus, necessitated by personal economic difficulties.[7] These acquisitions were driven by his steadfast desire to build a collection that would encapsulate the most significant achievements of what he viewed as an unprecedented cultural movement taking shape around him. Dr. Panza, moreover, distinguished himself by purchasing works by younger artists before they had garnered substantial critical attention. As a result, he is recognized as one of the earliest supporters of now-renowned artists such as Hanne Darboven, Robert Irwin, and Sol LeWitt. In addition, the collector set himself the task of acquiring the work of certain artists in depth, resulting in a collection whose highlights include more than twenty wall drawings by Sol LeWitt, thirty sculptures by Richard Nonas, fifty-two text pieces by Lawrence Weiner, and forty-two works by Bruce Nauman, among others.[8] This growing collection was housed in the Panza's home in Varese, where galleries installed with multiple works by a single artist provide a focused overview of that individual's accomplishments. In addition, the Villa Panza became the setting for site-specific projects by Robert Irwin,

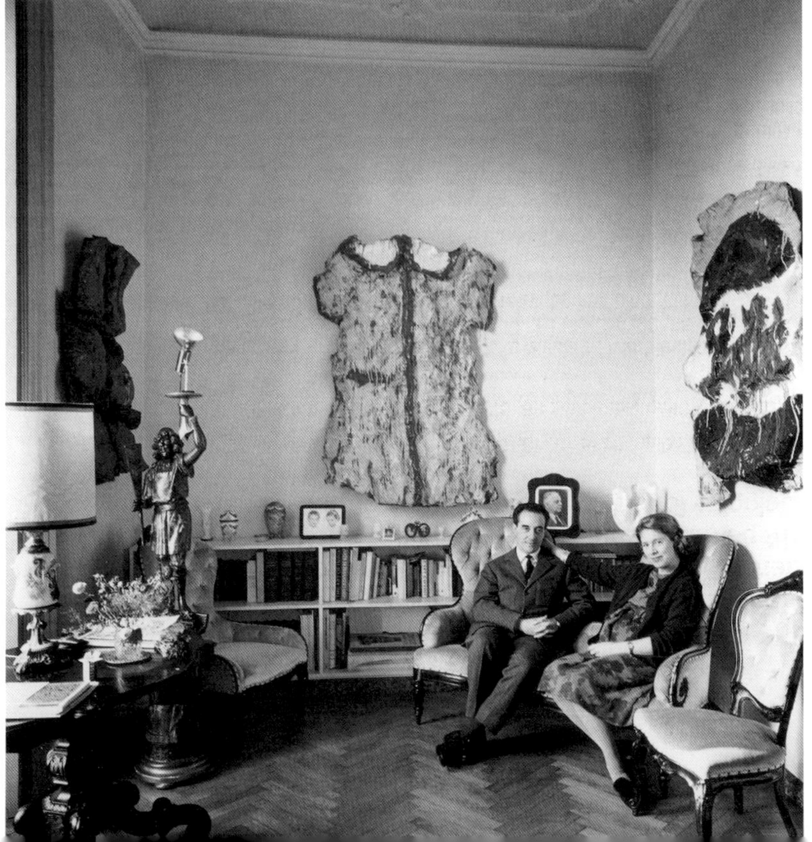

Dr. Giuseppe and Mrs. Giovanna Panza at the Villa Menafoglio Litta Panza, Varese, Italy, 1966

Dan Flavin, Maria Nordman, and James Turrell, offering dedicated, permanent spaces for art that was commercially unviable, inappropriate as museum acquisitions, or simply unsuitable for temporary installations.

Dr. Panza's intellectual curiosity is apparent in his embrace of artists who renounced the premises of works already in his collection. His willingness, moreover, to purchase art that was immaterial, site-specific, existed only as a set of written instructions, or was of such a large scale and complexity that it could never be realized in a domestic setting speaks to Dr. Panza's commitment to artistic endeavors that question the very proposition of collecting. Given the inherent complexities in acquiring art at this time, Dr. Panza proved himself to be particularly savvy in his negotiations with artists as he pursued their works. In the mid-1960s, artists began to generate certificates of authenticity and other documentation in order to clarify the process of transferring ownership of art that was essentially an idea; these contracts also often sought to guarantee artists the right to oversee the installation or refabrication of their works after they left the studio.[9] Dr. Panza, a lawyer by training, asserted his own rights by asking artists to sign a one-page, detailed agreement that verified the collector's sole ownership of the artwork in question, in some instances making the request years after a work had been purchased.[10] In the case of works that were re-created anew each time they were exhibited, such as Sol LeWitt's wall drawings or Doug Wheeler's room-sized light installations, Dr. Panza asked the artists to sign contracts that guaranteed the collector's right to realize the work repeatedly. Furthermore, Dr. Panza sought to redefine the authority of the collector by boldly requesting "the right to assemble them [works] without having to rely on the assistance of the artist," albeit theoretically subject to the artists' original instructions.[11]

The Hirshhorn Museum's Acquisition

By the late 1960s, the Panza Collection was renowned among dealers, artists, and curators, and Dr. Panza was identified with his avid pursuit of works for which few collectors had an appreciation. In addition to providing a view onto a groundbreaking era in the history of art, the Panza Collection, with its unparalleled scope and scale, carries historical value of another sort: many of the works from the 1960s and 1970s in the collection might not have been preserved or, in the case of large-scale and site-specific projects, might never

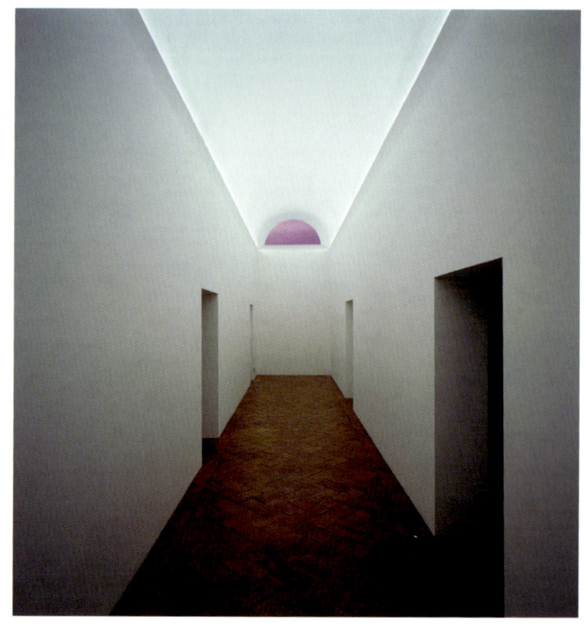

James Turrell
American, b. Los Angeles, California, 1943
Sky Window I, Varese 1976, 1976
Lunette cut into exterior wall
and fluorescent light
The Solomon R. Guggenheim Foundation,
New York – Panza Collection, Gift 1992,
permanent loan to FAI, Fondo per
l'Ambiente Italiano

have been realized if not for Dr. Panza's eagerness to acquire across a broad range of media and artistic practices. While there were other individuals actively purchasing contemporary American and European art during this period, such as Dorothy and Herbert Vogel, Phillipa de Menil and Heiner Friedrich, Irene and Peter Ludwig, and Edidio Marzona, the Panza Collection stands apart for its breadth and depth. Indeed, no collector during this era matched Dr. Panza's willingness to acquire so many important Conceptual works or site-specific and large-scale installations. Moreover, most museums at this time were either unwilling or unable to risk the means required to collect untraditional media, whether Conceptual works that existed only in documentary certificates, site-specific projects that permanently occupied valuable gallery space, or room-sized environments that required vast amounts of storage space and significant resources to install with each iteration. Forty years later, however, many of the works in the Panza Collection are now valued as canonical examples of post-Greenbergian artistic production and, therefore, are highly sought after by both museums and private collectors. Dr. Panza, meanwhile, has focused much of his attention in recent years to transferring his holdings to museums such as the Hirshhorn in order to ensure that these works will be available to international audiences.

The thirty-nine works acquired by the Hirshhorn from the Panza Collection give an overview of the critical premises driving Conceptual, Minimal, Light and Space, and Environmental art in the late 1960s and early 1970s. As a group, these works attest to the remarkable diversity of artistic practices that flourished amidst a wide-ranging interrogation of the nature and meaning of art. And in many instances, the works here signify these artists' most important early innovations. Moreover, in the case of artists represented by multiple works, such as Robert Irwin and Joseph Kosuth, the Hirshhorn's collection now provides an overview of those individuals' development during a critical period in both their careers and the history of contemporary art.

Conceptual Art and Language

Hailed as the first exhibition of what would soon become known as Conceptual Art, *January 5–31, 1969* at Seth Siegelaub's New York gallery brought together works by Robert Barry, Douglas Huebler, Joseph Kosuth, and Lawrence Weiner for the first time. These four artists focused attention on

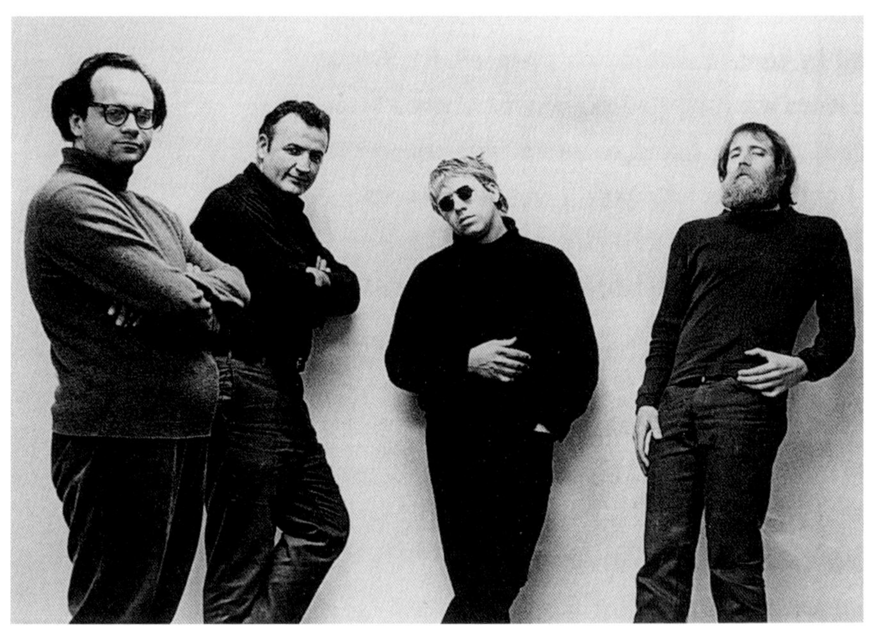

Robert Barry, Douglas Huebler, Joseph Kosuth, and Lawrence Weiner at *January 5–31, 1969* exhibition organized by Seth Siegelaub. Courtesy The Siegelaub Collection and Archives

the paramount role that philosophy could play in the visual arts with works predicated on the primacy of language. By requiring gallery visitors to read a text rather than view a handcrafted object, these artists flouted the conventions for engaging a work of art.[12]

A prolific writer deeply interested in philosophy, Joseph Kosuth established himself as a formidable presence in the New York art world in the mid-1960s with text-based works that questioned the processes of signification, particularly the arbitrary relationship between language and the objects and ideas it represents. The five works that the Hirshhorn acquired from the Panza Collection provide an overview of Kosuth's most salient early projects. The neon *Self-Defined*, 1965, and the glass *Box, Cube, Empty, Clear, Glass—a Description*, 1965, announced Kosuth's rejection of conventional media and introduced the tactic of juxtaposing material and text in order to suggest how each creates meaning, both independently and in conjunction with one another. With the *Proto-Investigations* series, Kosuth expanded his inquiry by introducing another signifying system: photography. *'One and Five (Clock) [Eng.-Ita.]'*, 1965, for example, displays a common clock with a similarly scaled photograph and appropriated dictionary definitions of "clock," "time," and "object." Kosuth, however, was dissatisfied with imagery that is irrevocably attached to physical objects and photographs, so he began to exhibit only the mechanically reproduced dictionary entries, which comprise his most famous body of work, *'Titled (Art as Idea as Idea)'*. Bracketed by the legacy of Duchamp's readymades and Ad Reinhardt's claim that "art is art-as-art and everything else is everything else," Kosuth's *'Titled (Art as Idea as Idea) [idea]'*, 1966, and *'Titled (Art as Idea as Idea) [ultimate]'*, 1967, assert the primacy of idea over material as well as the central role that language could play in the production of visual art.[13]

The next year, Lawrence Weiner formulated the following precepts for his artistic practice:

> 1. The artist may construct the piece
> 2. The piece may be fabricated
> 3. The piece need not be built
>
> Each being equal and consistent with the intent of the artist the decision as to condition rests with the receiver upon the occasion of receivership.[14]

Sketch for Joseph Kosuth's *'One and Five (Clock) [Eng.-Ita.]'*, 1965

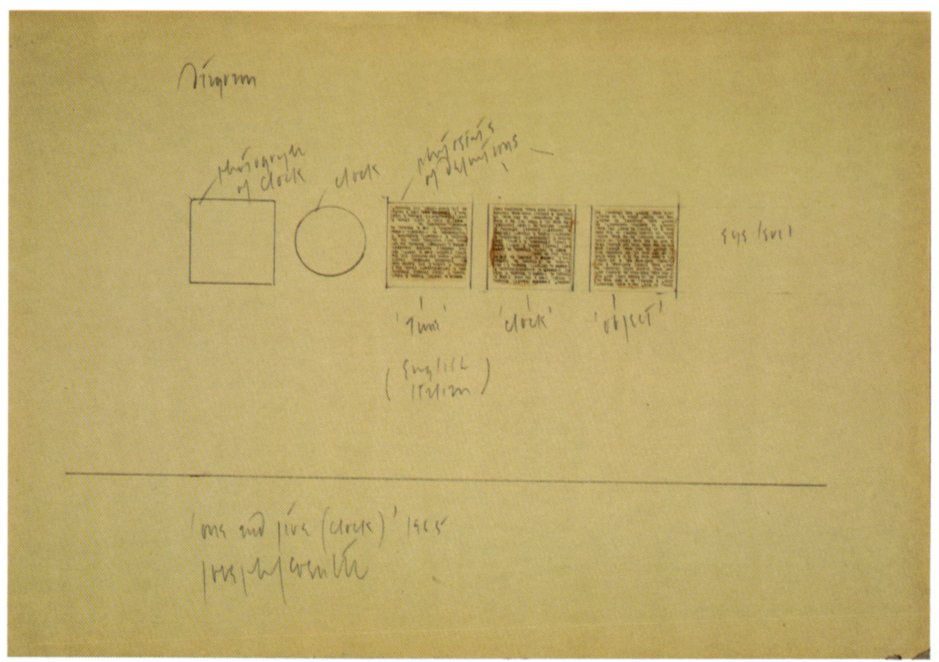

Since then, Weiner's work has consisted solely of what he calls "statements": words, clauses, and phrases that, according to the above directives, may be realized in any format (written or spoken), in any context, by anyone—or not at all. An art without formal parameters or tangible objects, Weiner's practice seems to suggest a process based on a sort of pure idealism; in fact, each of Weiner's works is grounded in the empirical, observable world, whether actions, materials, or places.[15] Devoid of context and voice, pieces such as *REDUCED, Cat. No. 102*, 1970, and *A rubber ball thrown on the sea, Cat. No. 146*, 1969, are not meant to be illustrative of a discrete action or moment; rather, they are designed to conjure up a potentially infinite array of references that are circumscribed only by the reader and the works' presentation, both of which are outside the artist's purview. By relinquishing all responsibility for installation, Weiner encouraged his texts' appearance in both traditional gallery spaces and more atypical locations, such as matchbooks, water towers, lighthouses, manhole covers, and as tattoos on the body. Indelibly elastic, Weiner's statements explore the contingency of language while at the same time transcending the limited existence of tangible objects.

In the late 1960s, Robert Barry reconsidered the nature of visual art by producing works in unconventional media that explored the intangible and invisible, from the phenomena that frame our physical existence to the semantic systems that govern the ways we communicate.[16] His early *Steel Disc Suspended 1/8 in. Above Floor*, 1967, is a tangible object; nevertheless, the work's nylon filament is all but transparent, generating the illusion of a disc hovering beyond the reach of gravity. When he started to create equivocal texts such as *It Can Only Be Known as Something Else*, 1969, Barry revealed his predilection for ideas over palpable objects. *It...*, 1969–71, one of a series of text-based slide projections, pushed the limits of representation even further by employing the fugitive medium of light. *It...* comprises sixty slides (fifty-nine with texts, one blank) spaced at eight-second intervals. Each slide features an elusive "it" as the subject, which encourages, or even requires, viewers to draw their own conclusions about the texts' subjects (which may or may not include art).

In 1968, two years after earning recognition for sculptures shown in the

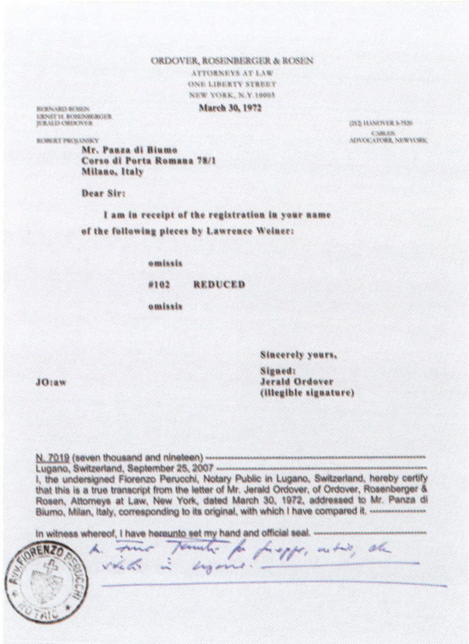

ORDOVER, ROSENBERGER & ROSEN
ATTORNEYS AT LAW
ONE LIBERTY STREET
NEW YORK, N.Y. 10005

BERNARD ROSEN
ERNST H. ROSENBERGER
JERALD ORDOVER
ROBERT PROJANSKY

CABLES
ADVOCATORR, NEWYORK

March 30, 1972

Mr. Panza di Biumo
Corso di Porta Romana 78/1
Milano, Italy

Dear Sir:

I am in receipt of the registration in your name of the following pieces by Lawrence Weiner:

omissis

#102 REDUCED

omissis

Sincerely yours,

Signed:
Jerald Ordover
(illegible signature)

JO:aw

N. 7019 (seven thousand and nineteen) ----------
Lugano, Switzerland, September 25, 2007 ----------
I, the undersigned Fiorenzo Perucchi, Notary Public in Lugano, Switzerland, hereby certify that this is a true transcript from the letter of Mr. Jerald Ordover, of Ordover, Rosenberger & Rosen, Attorneys at Law, New York, dated March 30, 1972, addressed to Mr. Panza di Biumo, Milan, Italy, corresponding to its original, with which I have compared it. ----------

In witness whereof, I have hereunto set my hand and official seal. ----------

Certificate of ownership for Lawrence Weiner's *REDUCED, Cat. No. 102*, 1970

landmark Minimalist exhibition *Primary Structures*, Douglas Huebler rejected three-dimensional object-making altogether and began to produce series of photographic snapshots that ostensibly "picture" the prosaic and often absurd actions described in the accompanying captions.[17] Huebler examines how process and perception play out over the interval during which an artist creates a work, as well as the time that the viewer subsequently experiences it. *Variable Piece #4 New York City*, 1968, for example, features ten black-and-white photographs of a New York intersection that the artist shot with his eyes closed; the caption, by contrast, describes a situation wherein Huebler invited Jewish Museum visitors to participate in "the transposition of information from one location to another" by transcribing a never-revealed secret and exchanging it for one previously submitted. Balancing a Dada-like sensibility with a set of self-imposed conceptual limits, the artist offers astute observations about the ways that stereotypes and other socially constructed systems delineate our experiences. *Duration Piece #12 Venice, California—Plum Island (Newbury Port), Massachusetts*, 1969, which describes the transporting of sand across land and sea between beaches in California and Massachusetts, likewise offers a pairing of text and image that presents itself as ordered by an underlying system that nevertheless remains elusive or even overtly subjective. As a group, Huebler's works suggest how linguistic description overrides photography's professed capacity for mimesis ultimately to determine our understanding of events and the images that represent them.

Minimal Forms

The logical, predetermined systems and spare, repeated forms that are the hallmark of Sol LeWitt's long career provided a nexus between Conceptual and Minimal art. In 1967, the artist published in *Artforum* "Paragraphs on Conceptual Art," which enumerated the basic tenets driving his work as well as that of a number of his peers: idea over execution and craftsmanship, plans and systems rather than subjectivity, and a disavowal of illustration.[18] The following year, LeWitt applied these principles to the problem of creating a truly two-dimensional drawing, one that was executed directly on a wall without any intervening support, such as canvas or paper.[19] LeWitt revolutionized the medium's conventions by proposing an ephemeral, mural-sized drawing structured by an elemental

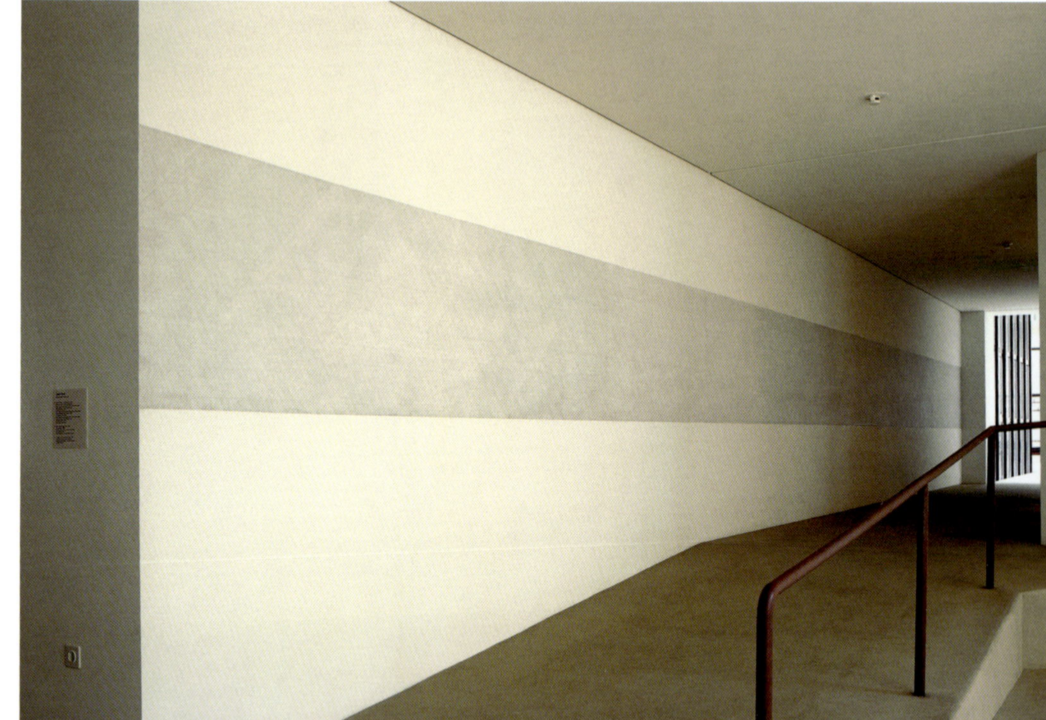

combination of lines that would be repeated until the designated site, not necessarily chosen by the artist, was filled. When one of his drawings was purchased, LeWitt provided a brief, carefully worded set of instructions, along with a schematic diagram of one possible variation of the primary design unit; the drawing was not realized by the artist himself, but rather by others, who would adapt his instructions as they saw fit to suit the parameters of each space. *Wall Drawing #3*, first installed in 1969, exemplifies the unexpected subtlety of the earliest of LeWitt's wall drawings, in which the hand-drawn, graphite lines read as both materially distinct from and continuous with the underlying and surrounding surfaces. While his wall drawings would eventually include a wide variety of colors and shapes, it was in these earliest pencil drawings that the artist established his distinctive balance between proscribed formulas, serial repetition, and open-ended, idiosyncratic variations.

While many artists in the Hirshhorn's acquisition from the Panza Collection built upon the Minimalist ideas of Donald Judd and his colleagues, Richard Nonas's use of deceptively reductive forms and industrial materials to modify perceptions of the surrounding environment brings him closest to their work. Nevertheless, Nonas, like his contemporaries Marc di Suvero and Richard Serra, dispensed with Judd's exacting precision and pristine surfaces in favor of elements that had a more patent physicality, such as rough-hewn wood and weather-beaten steel. Composed of simple, architectonic forms assembled in a seemingly casual manner, Nonas's sculptures belie the complexity of their creation and effect, which relies upon sophisticated refinements in scale, proportion, and weight to heighten the objects' physical presence. The steel floorpiece *Salita Nord #2 (Fault Line)*, 1974, exemplifies the way in which Nonas's sculptures deftly inhabit a given space, occupying the floor with a monolithic presence that is nevertheless subverted by the work's haphazardly overlapping forms and irregular surfaces. *Genoa Slot Series (1 Down 1 Up)*, 1974, a smaller-scale wall piece, similarly breaks the expanse of the surface on which it is mounted, even as it reveals a sliver of its white background, thereby reasserting the sculpture's interrelationship with the neighboring architecture. Nonas's range of media and scale notwithstanding, the artist's practice is unified by an ongoing scrutiny of how individual forms and materials interact

Installation view of
Sol LeWitt's *Wall Drawing #3*,
1969

with one another and the surrounding environment, thereby foregrounding the viewers' perception of spatial relationships.

Light and Space

Working in Los Angeles in the late 1960s and early 1970s, Robert Irwin, Doug Wheeler, and Larry Bell created large-scale sculptures and room-sized installations that drew on the science of optics and, in particular, the processes of perception. Rather than forming a cohesive group or movement, these artists are connected by their use of modern materials to create ephemeral visual effects; their work, however, also suggests the influence of the region's distinctive climate, as well as the growing presence of the aerospace and entertainment industries during this period.[20]

For more than forty years, Robert Irwin has called attention to phenomenological experiences with elegant pieces that subtly undermine their own presence. The three objects acquired by the Hirshhorn represent Irwin's most notable early efforts, which not only provided the critical groundwork for much of the artist's subsequent practice, but also established him as an influential artist, teacher, and theoretician. *Untitled*, 1963–65, is from one of Irwin's final painting series, which questioned the materiality of painting and the limits of perception. *Untitled* features tiny, hand-painted red and green dots juxtaposed in varying densities across the surface of the canvas, so that, from a distance, the complementary hues cancel each other out, dispensing with the conventional image-ground relationship in favor of an ostensibly blank, bulging canvas. Irwin soon abandoned painting but continued these early optical experiments with a series of convex aluminum discs sprayed with concentric circles of almost imperceptibly modulated acrylic paint.[21] Hung away from the wall and lit with four lights that cast a rosette shadow, *Untitled*, 1966–67, appears to transcend the physical boundaries of the aluminum and merge with the adjacent wall. Several years later, Irwin fabricated a series of untitled columns using a special optical acrylic that approximates the clarity of crystal.[22] Embedded directly into the floor, these twelve-foot, triangular columns create spectacular effects that range from casting a full color spectrum to becoming completely transparent, depending on the lighting and viewer's vantage point at a particular moment.

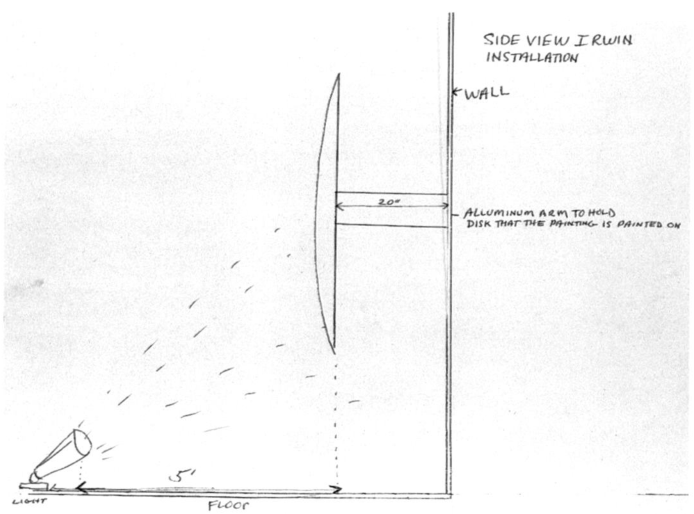

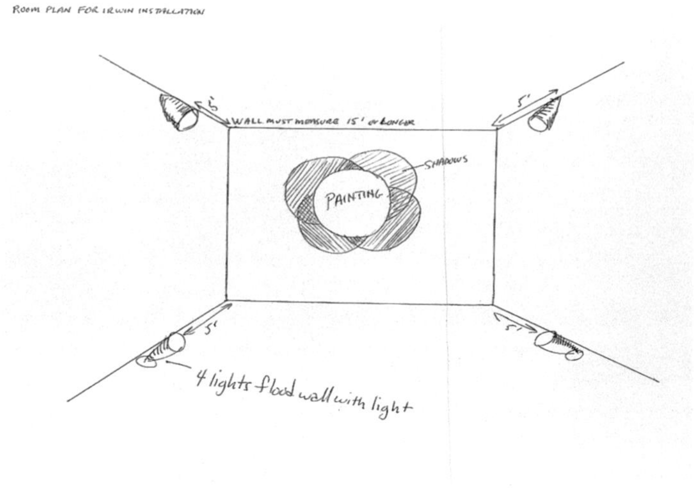

Doug Wheeler likewise sought to thwart viewers' assumptions about the nature of art and perception with room-size environments that foregrounded purely optical experiences. Wheeler, who ascribes his interest in working with light to time spent in the Arizona desert, first garnered attention in the mid-1960s for his "encasements," painted plastic squares illuminated from behind by commercial neon tubing.[23] Hung on the wall, these early objects launched Wheeler's exploration of light by questioning the essential qualities and limits of painting. By 1969, Wheeler had started to construct large-scale, theatrical light installations, including *Eindhoven, Environmental Light Installation*, 1969, a project initially exhibited at the Van Abbemuseum in The Netherlands. *Eindhoven* takes the form of an enclosed room accessed by two ramps; the focal point is the far wall, where four coves containing white neon lighting fixtures trace the points where the walls, ceiling, and floor intersect. With the neon tubes concealed, visitors are presented with a glowing, frame-like form of reflected light. Wheeler's installations, like the work of Irwin, displaced the Minimalist predilection for physically assertive objects in favor of intangible artworks that confronted viewers with their own perceptual processes.

While Irwin and Wheeler moved towards the immaterial, Larry Bell, by contrast, confounded expectations of the viewing experience with large-scale, glass sculptures that defiantly declared their corporeality even as they created the illusion of a continuum with the surrounding space. In the mid-1960s, Bell adopted a commercial vacuum-coating process to cover glass panes with tiny particles of metal alloy, resulting in a uniform surface of evanescent color that is equally transparent and reflective. Initially, Bell produced small cubes placed on acrylic pedestals, but, by 1968, he had moved to large freestanding sculptures composed of two or more glass walls placed at varying angles.[24] At once an ominous presence and a dizzying entertainment spectacle, *Untitled*, 1973, exemplifies the ways Bell's monumental sculptures obscured traditional object-subject relations by allowing visitors to view his installation while simultaneously observing both their own reflections and the actions of their fellow gallery visitors on the other side of the work.

Time/Duration

In the 1960s, On Kawara, Roman Opalka, and Hanne Darboven each

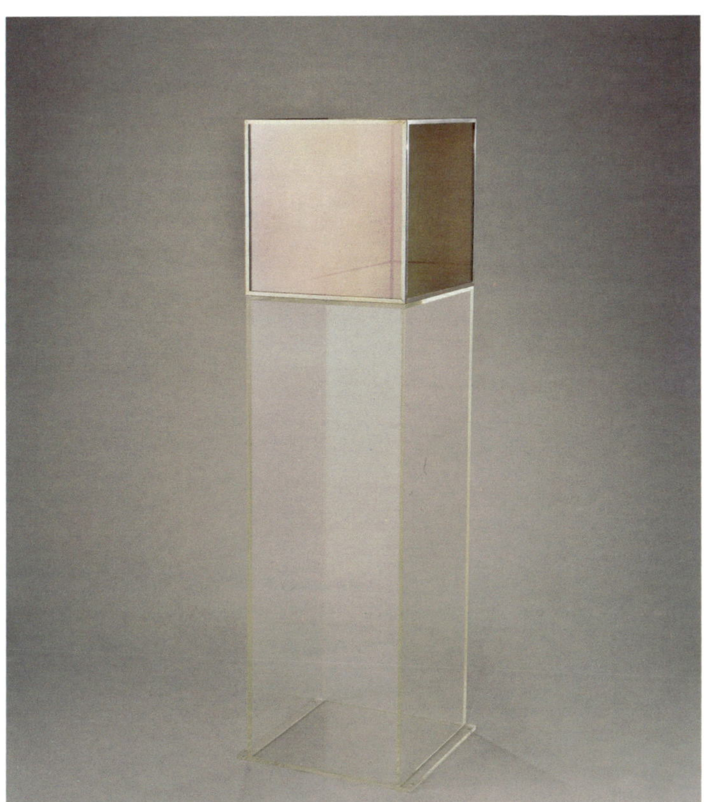

THIS PAGE
Larry Bell
American, b. Chicago, Illinois, 1939
Untitled, 1964
Glass, bismuth, chromium, gold, and rhodium on gold-plated brass
54¼ × 16⅜ × 14¼ inches
The Joseph H. Hirshhorn Bequest, 1981 (86.294)

OPPOSITE
Installation instructions for Robert Irwin's *Untitled*, 1966–67

developed distinctive methods of visually representing the universal yet elusive concept of time. Despite their individual preoccupations, these three artists come together through their process-driven approaches and lifelong commitments to serial projects that verge on obsession. Importantly, Kawara, Opalka, and Darboven, unlike so many artists of their generation, did not disavow painting and drawing; rather, they abandoned traditional modes of representation, instead devising systems to manifest the passage of time.

The three paintings by On Kawara acquired by the Hirshhorn—*Oct. 24, 1971*, *Oct. 26, 1971*, and *Oct. 29, 1971*, all 1971—are all from his *Today Series,* an ongoing project that the artist began in January 1966 and that now comprises more than 2,000 monochrome paintings, each documenting the date on which it was created. Deceptively cool and straightforward, Kawara's date paintings actually are the result of a strictly proscribed, painstaking process. Each work is executed on a pre-stretched, horizontal canvas that conforms to one of eight sizes, ranging from approximately 8 × 10 inches to 61 × 88½ inches. The artist applies four or five coats of a deeply saturated, acrylic paint; after each layer dries, it is then sanded down to create a matte surface devoid of brushwork. In the center of each canvas, Kawara carefully writes the date, using multiple layers of white paint, in the language and format of the country where the work is made.[25] If a painting is not finished by midnight of the day it was started, Kawara destroys it. Each completed painting is kept in a cardboard box, along with a page from a local newspaper published that same day, representing the complex relationship between the abstract concepts driving the artist's solitary project and concurrent events of daily life. Kawara's *One Million Years*, 1970–71, a ten-volume set of typewritten notebooks filled with columns of the years between 998031 BC and AD 1969 similarly reminds us of our comparably brief existence.

Roman Opalka likewise embarked upon a lifelong project that measures the passage of time in paint; Opalka, however, set himself the unattainable

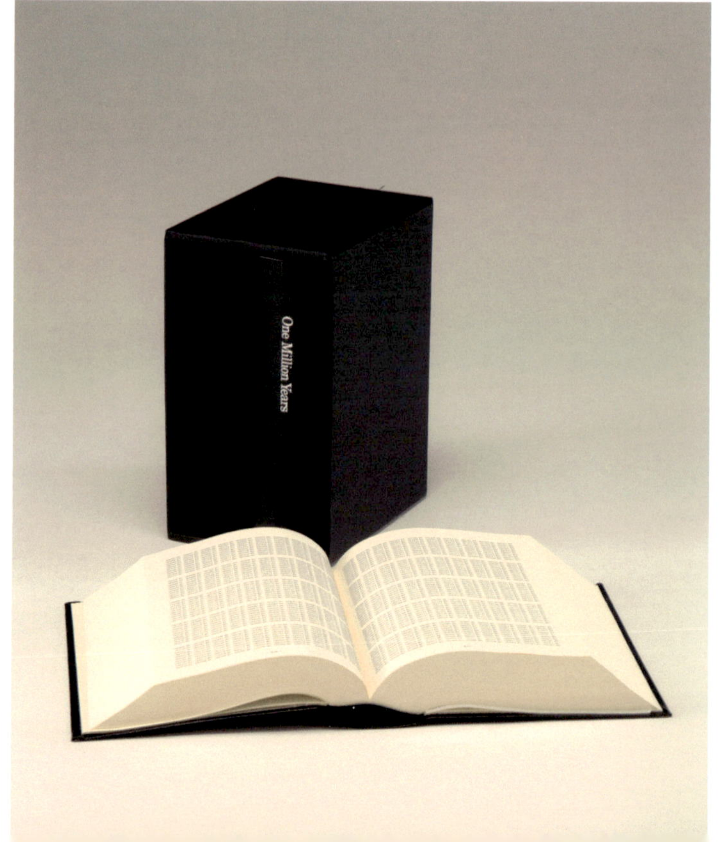

On Kawara
Japanese, b. Kariya, 1933
One Million Years—For the Last One—For All Those Who Have Lived and Died 42/60, 1999
Printed multiple; two signed volumes, 2,001 pages each
6⅜ × 3½ × 4⅜ inches
Gift of Giuseppe Panza, 2007 (07.100)

goal of counting from one to infinity. Since 1965, the artist has painted only large (77 × 53¼ inches) canvases, each laden with a long sequence of numbers that begins in the top left corner and progresses left to right, line by line, top to bottom. Working on a dark ground, Opalka draws the numbers with white acrylic paint, refilling the brush only when it is depleted of pigment.[26] The resulting painting, such as *1965/1–∞: Detail 460260–484052*, begun 1965, features an irregular pattern of surging gray and white tones, which offsets the plodding regularity of the counting process.[27] At the same time, Opalka's handwriting grows larger and more uncertain as the artist tires from the monotonous labor that constitutes each eight-hour workday. In 1968, Opalka began to record himself speaking the numbers in his native Polish as he wrote them and, moreover, to photograph himself at the end of each day.[28] Together, Opalka's paintings and photographs offer an intimate portrait of the passing of an individual life against the relentless march of time.

Seeking "a way of writing without describing,"[29] Hanne Darboven rejected existing calendrical conventions and developed her own system of signs to chronicle the course of time. In the late 1960s, Darboven initiated a daily practice of writing, methodically filling sheet after sheet of paper with her distinctive graphic lexicon, which has come to include numbers, words, musical and scientific notations, unintelligible script, and fragments of personal and collective history. Many of Darboven's early pieces, including the typed *27K-No8-No26*, 1968–69, and the handwritten *00-99=No1-2K-20K,* 1969–70, are structured by a numerical system derived from the digits that make up a particular date: January 1, 2008 becomes 1+1+0+8=10 and December 31, 2008 becomes 12+31+0+8=51. (The first two digits of the year are always expunged, and, often, a K is added to signify "sum.") Using a seemingly idiosyncratic, yet rigorous procedure, Darboven then progresses through a series of mathematical permutations and patterns that, as a group, give visual form to both the orderly progress of time and the unpredictable flux of life. The resulting compendiums offer a written

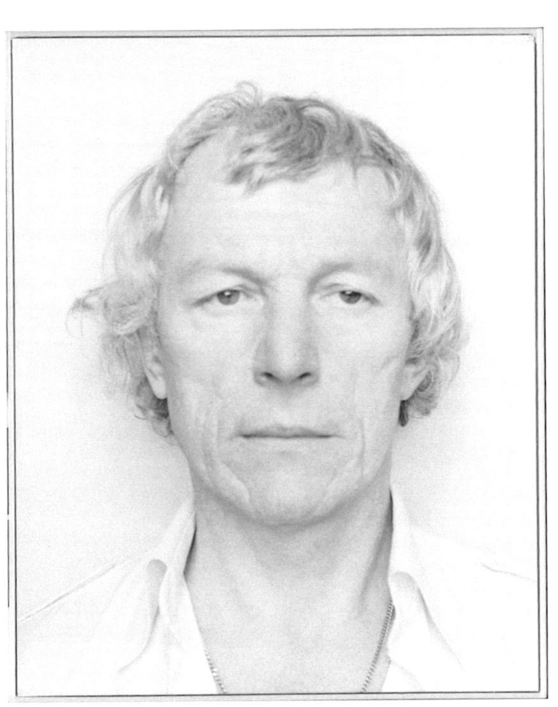

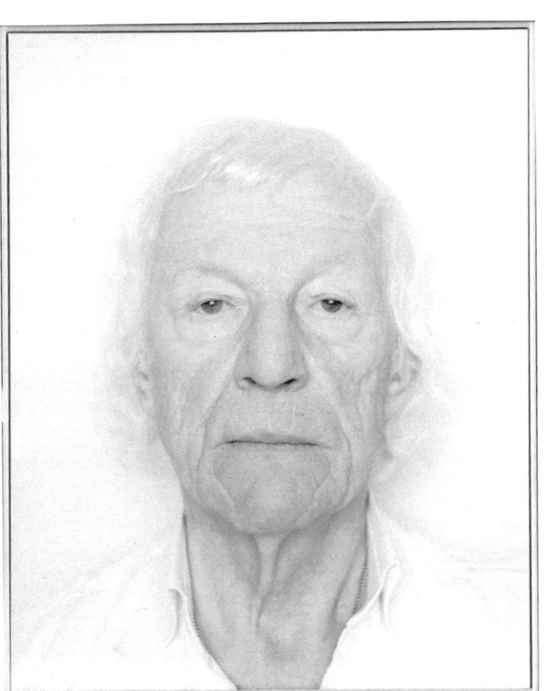

LEFT TO RIGHT

Roman Opalka
Polish, b. Abbeville, France, 1931
1965/1–∞ Detail 2382351, after 1965
Gelatin silver print and artist's frame
12¼ × 9½ × 1 inches, framed
Gift of Giuseppe Panza, 2007 (07.101)

Roman Opalka
Polish, b. Abbeville, France, 1931
1965/1–∞ Detail 5122577, after 1965
Gelatin silver print and artist's frame
12¼ × 9½ × 1 inches, framed
Gift of Giuseppe Panza, 2007 (07.102)

record of the historical interval enumerated by Darboven as well as the duration that it took the artist to complete the work, which are re-activated into the present with each subsequent act of viewing.

Nature/Landscape

As many American and European artists in the late 1960s rejected conventional subjects, Richard Long, Hamish Fulton, and Jan Dibbets instead made art that drew inspiration from or reconsidered one of the most traditional subjects: nature. Richard Long's multi-faceted practice includes sculptures, drawings, photographs, and texts that stem from his experiences walking through the landscape. In 1967, Long constructed *A Line Made By Walking*, a straight path through a grass field, which inaugurated his series of outdoor ephemeral forms crafted from such available sources as mud, sticks, and stones. An alternative to both existing outdoor memorials and studio-based approaches, Long's sculptures feature elemental forms—lines, spirals, and circles—that suggest the artist's wanderings over a distance and period of time. Long's formal vocabulary, however, is powerful in its multivalence, as his choice of spare, geometric structures that are common to many cultures also opens a dialogue with the tenets of Minimalism, albeit employing natural rather than industrial materials. Long initially exhibited photographs and maps that documented his movements outdoors. As demand for his art increased, the artist began to make sculptures using objects and matter gathered at sites he had traversed. Decidedly less ephemeral and more commercially viable, works such as *Carrara Line*, 1985, nevertheless uphold Long's essential praxis:[30] the solitary process of walking is Long's art, while the objects produced either during or after the journey offer a distillation, or index, of both personal experience and place.[31]

Since the early 1970s, the art of Hamish Fulton, like that of Richard Long, has been circumscribed by the activity of trekking through rural spaces. While the two artists share an overarching commitment to process and a direct, almost romantic engagement with the landscape, Fulton eschewed

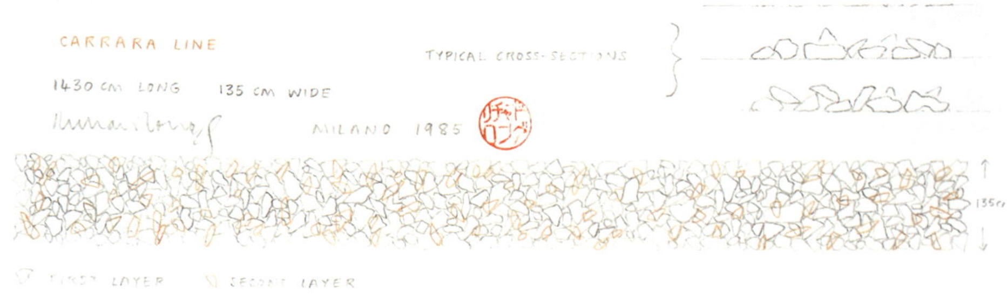

the creation of objects in-situ or the use of natural elements in favor of photographic images and printed texts. In choosing the medium of photography, Fulton directly challenged Western landscape conventions, such as the pastoral or sublime, as well as the idea that a photograph could provide a document of a location or encounter. Instead, Fulton's photographs call attention to the contingency of experience and the uneasy relationship between the camera and the subjects it purports to represent.[32] The two-part *Facing Both Ways*, 1972, for example, offers opposing views of the surrounding landscape at a particular moment, an allusion to the impossibility of ever recovering, or even conveying, the totality of a site or event in anything more than a series of subjective fragments. *France on the Horizon*, 1975, provides a more conventional, picturesque view across the English Channel, which the artist photographed one morning during a walk; nevertheless, Fulton's caption—"France on the horizon/21 miles across the Channel/a one day 50 mile walk by way of the White Cliffs of Dover/early summer 1975"—evokes the web of historical, art historical, geographic, and personal associations that inform both the artist's interpretation of this specific place and the photograph that ultimately fails at representation.

In the late 1960s, Jan Dibbets also used photographs to explore the nexus between the medium and nature. Often grouped with Long and Fulton, whom the artist met in 1967 while an art student in London, Dibbets was less concerned with landscape, per se, than with the ways in which we perceive the world around us, particularly how photography structures visual experience as it unfolds over time.[33] Importantly, Dibbets, who first trained and exhibited as a painter, also stood apart from other conceptual photographers, such as Douglas Huebler or even Hamish Fulton, by evincing an abiding interest in aesthetics. The eighty-photograph sequence *The Shortest Day of 1970 Photographed in My House Every 6 Minutes from Sunrise til Sunset*, 1970, which captures the movement of daylight from a fixed position, exemplifies Dibbets' unique commingling of conceptual and formal

Installation instructions
for Richard Long's
Carrara Line, 1985

concerns. Essentially a catalogue of an empty room's inactivity, Dibbets' photographic grid invokes Dutch painting precedents ranging from Vermeer through Mondrian to pose questions about space, temporality, and the camera's role in giving narrative structure to a series of events.[34] *Flood Tide*, 1969, likewise records the unremitting cycle of waves in an incoming tide as it gradually overtakes a perpendicular channel drawn in the sand.

The Body

Like the other Conceptual artists whose work Dr. Panza collected, Bruce Nauman is staunchly committed to producing art that defies conventions. Nauman has produced psychologically riveting, highly enigmatic works in a broad range of media, including wax, neon, fiberglass, film, video, photography, performance, and installations. Over the last forty years, his subjects—the body, language, the human condition, and the nature of studio practice, among others—have varied as widely as his materials; nevertheless, his output is anchored by the fundamental conviction that idea and process outweigh the resulting object. The pivotal early film *Art Make-Up #1–4*, 1967–68, exemplifies Nauman's pioneering approach to art-making at a moment when the artist was using his own body as both subject and object.[35] One of a number of films featuring Nauman performing monotonous, repetitive acts, *Art Make-Up #1–4* shows the artist applying white, pink, green, and black stage make-up in succession to his body. Nauman's rehearsal of the masking activity that normally precedes a film or theatrical production calls attention to the way in which a visual artist's identity or presence plays out in his or her work.[36] Screened as four synchronized projections on the walls of the gallery, the work surrounds viewers, challenging them to consider their own participation in the creation of any art object.

•

The thirty-nine works acquired by the Hirshhorn, while only a fraction of the Panza Collection, nevertheless suggest a dedicated collector at once steadfast and audacious enough to acquire hundreds of artworks in the face of a radical reconsideration of both the parameters of art and the roles of artists, viewers, and collectors. Dr. Panza's eagerness to ensure that these important works are available to future generations by placing them in public institutions such as the Hirshhorn Museum and Sculpture Garden reflects his ongoing commitment to the art of this period, as well as his acute understanding of its significance within the trajectory of twentieth-century artistic practices. As part of the Hirshhorn's collection, these works will offer museum visitors new perspectives on not only the art of this particular historical moment, but also the ways contemporary artists continue both to draw on and reconsider the ideas of a preceding generation.

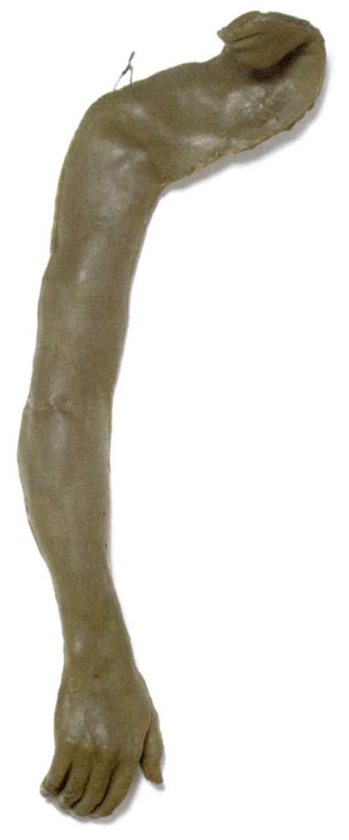

Bruce Nauman
American, b. Fort Wayne, Indiana, 1941
From Hand To Mouth, 1967
Wax over cloth
28 × 10⅛ × 4 inches
Joseph H. Hirshhorn Purchase Fund, Holenia Purchase Fund, in memory of Joseph H. Hirshhorn, and Museum Purchase, 1993 (93.6)

Notes

1 Walter Benjamin, "Unpacking my Library: A Talk about Book Collecting," in *Illuminations*, ed. Hannah Arendt (New York: Schocken Books, 1969), 60. Joseph Kosuth, "Art After Philosophy," in *Art After Philosophy and After: Collected Writings, 1966–1990*, ed. Gabriel Guercio (Cambridge and London: The MIT Press, 1991), 18. Originally published in Arthur R. Rose, "Four Interviews," *Arts Magazine* 43, no. 4 (February 1969), 23.

2 The corridor is also the site of a commissioned installation by Dan Flavin, *Varese Corridor*, which comprises two rows of neon lights running the length of the hall. The Flavin installation, when illuminated, prevents visitors from properly viewing the works in the adjoining galleries, so it is switched on only for a few moments at a time. Lucia Borromeo Dina, "Dan Flavin's Installations at the Villa Panza: Problems Raised by their Display and Maintenance," in *Dan Flavin: Rooms of Light* (Milan: Skira, 2004), 45.

3 Figure based on interview between Mitchell P. Rales and Dr. Panza, July 2008. 2,500 represents the Panza Collection as a whole. In 1984, Dr. Panza sold eighty works, primarily examples of Abstract Expressionist, Color Field, and Pop art, to the Museum of Contemporary Art, Los Angeles; in 1994, he donated seventy pieces produced by Los Angeles–based artists in the late 1980s and 1990s to MOCA. In 1991, the Solomon R. Guggenheim Museum of Art in New York acquired by purchase and donation 350 works by Southern California artists from the 1960s and 1970s. More recently, Dr. Panza donated works to the Museo Cantonale d'Arte in Lugano, Switzerland, and placed works on long-term loan with the Ducal Palace in Gubbio and the Mart, the Museum of Modern and Contemporary Art of Rovereto and Trento in Italy. In addition, his villa in Varese opened to the public as a historic property and museum in 2000.

4 Dr. Panza collected pieces by artists working outside the United States; however, the bulk of his collection is by American artists. In the aftermath of World War II, "America was a return to life," according to Dr. Panza. "This was one of the reasons that [American art] provoked a stronger interest in its new cultural message. At the end of the day it had superceded Europe in everything." Giuseppe Panza, *Memories of a Collector*, trans. Michael Haggerty (New York and London: Abbeville Press Publishers, 2007), 79, 85.

5 Panza, *Memories of a Collector*, 80.

6 Clement Greenberg, "Modernist Painting," in *Clement Greenberg: The Collected Essays and Criticism: Volume 4, Modernism with a Vengeance, 1957–1969*, ed. John O'Brian (Chicago and London: The University of Chicago Press, 1986), 86.

7 Dr. Panza's first break from collecting occurred between 1963 and 1969. Economic instability once again prompted Dr. Panza to take a second break from collecting between 1976 and 1989. Since 1989, Dr. Panza has assembled a collection of smaller-scale, abstract paintings, primarily by American artists. Christopher Knight, "Oral History with Count Giuseppe Panza di Biumo," April 2–4, 1985, Archives of American Art, Smithsonian Institution. Panza, *Memories of a Collector*, 231–36.

8 *Art of the Sixties and Seventies: The Panza Collection* (New York: Rizzoli, 1987), 145–259.

9 In 1971, Seth Siegelaub, the dealer who promoted such Conceptual artists as Joseph Kosuth and Lawrence Weiner, developed The Artists Reserved Rights Transfer and Sale Agreement. The contract, among other things, gives artists the right to share in the profits if a work was resold, making it the model document for artists seeking control over their work after it left their studio. In Dr. Panza's case, the voluminous correspondence between the collector, artists, and dealers indicates the complexities and, in some cases, the protracted negotiations that took place around the sale of an artwork. See Giuseppe Panza Papers, 1956–1990, Accession no. 940004, Getty Research Institute, Research Library, Los Angeles.

10 In his biography, Dr. Panza acknowledges the role that Jerald Ordover, "the lawyer for the Castelli Gallery and of many artists," played in drafting
a contract that, in his view, "is thorough and meets the needs of everybody and, above all, of art." Panza, *Memories of a Collector*, 138. For examples of Dr. Panza's contract, see Giuseppe Panza Papers, Box 123, Folder 1; Box 159, Folder 2.

11 Panza, *Memories of a Collector*, 137. Several artists, including Robert Irwin, agreed to sign Panza's contract only after making modifications that they felt protected the unique nature of their work. Giuseppe Panza Papers, Box 115, Folder 2.

12 *Conceptual Art*, ed. Peter Osborne (New York: Phaidon Press, 2002), 27.

13 Several authors have discussed Kosuth's deep engagement with Duchamp and Reinhardt. See Alexander Alberro, *Conceptual Art and the Politics of Publicity* (Cambridge and London: The MIT Press, 2004), 26–53, and Anne Rorimer, "Joseph Kosuth," in Ann Goldstein and Anne Rorimer, *Reconsidering the Object of Art: 1965–1975* (Cambridge and London: The Museum of Contemporary Art, Los Angeles, 1995), 150–51.

14 Lawrence Weiner in *January 5–31, 1969*, exhibition catalogue (New York: Seth Siegelaub, 1969). Cited in Lawrence Weiner, "[Statement of Intent]," in *Having Been Said: Writings & Interviews of Lawrence Weiner 1968–2003*, ed. Gerti Fietzek and Gregor Stemmrich (Ostfildern-Ruit: Hatje Cantz Verlag, 2004), 21.

15 His lack of interest in fabricated objects notwithstanding, Weiner repeatedly asserted, "Art is and must be an empirical reality concerned with the relationships of human beings to objects and objects to objects in relation to human beings." Lawrence Weiner, "Portraits: Section 2," *Artforum* 20, no. 9 (May 1982), 65, cited in Colin Gardner, "The Space between Words: Lawrence Weiner," *Artforum*, 29, no. 3 (November, 1990), 158.

16 Or, in Barry's words, "Nothing seems to me the most potent thing in the world." Tape recording of the February 8, 1968 symposium held in conjunction with the exhibition *Carl Andre, Robert Barry, Lawrence Weiner,* Bradford Junior College, Bradford, Massachusetts. Cited in Anne Rorimer, "Robert Barry," in Goldstein and Rorimer, *Reconsidering the Object of Art, 1965–1975*, 70.

17 Huebler famously stated in 1969, "The world is full of objects, more or less interesting; I do not wish to add any more." Douglas Huebler in *January 5–31, 1969*. Cited in *Douglas Huebler: Variable, Etc.* (New York: Distributed Art Publishers, 1993), 29.

18 Unlike many of his contemporaries, LeWitt never abandoned the conventional media of drawing and sculpture, though he did leave the interpretation and execution of his ideas to others. Sol LeWitt, "Paragraphs on Conceptual Art," *Artforum* 5, no. 10 (June 1967): 79–83.

19 "Sol LeWitt, June 12, 1969," in *Recording Conceptual Art: Early Interviews with Barry, Huebler, Kaltenbach, LeWitt, Morris, Oppenheim, Siegelaub, Smithson, Weiner*, eds. Alexander Alberro and Patricia Norvell (Berkeley: University of California Press, 2001), 113.

20 Germano Celant and Susan Cross, *Venice/Venezia: California Art from the Panza Collection at the Guggenheim* (New York: Solomon R. Guggenheim Museum, 2000), 42.

21 The Hirshhorn's collection also includes an acrylic disc painting *Untitled*, 1969, which Irwin produced soon after the aluminum discs.

22 Panza's archives include a document on Ace Gallery letterhead that details the fabrication specifications and effects of the acrylic columns. Giuseppe Panza Papers, Box 114, Folder 4.

23 Celant and Cross, *Venice/Venezia*, 88.

24 Bell's *Untitled*, 1964, in the Hirshhorn's collection is an example of the artist's smaller glass cube works.

25 Kawara's meticulous process produces the effect of a stencil; however, the artist uses only a ruler, set square, scalpel, and brushes. *Conceptual Art*, ed. Peter Osborne, 93.

26 Opalka started the project painting on a black ground. In 1972, when he reached 1,000,000, he began to add white to the background paint, increasing the quantity by one percent with each subsequent painting.

27 Opalka dates all of his works to 1965. Dates, however, are sometimes ascribed to paintings by others based on the numbers inscribed and, in the case of photographs, on the artist's appearance.

28 Dr. Panza donated two photographs by Opalka, *1965/1–∞: Detail 2382351* and *1965/1–∞: Detail 5122577*, to the Hirshhorn, but they do not relate directly to the painting in his collection.

29 Lucy Lippard, "Hanne Darboven: Deep in Numbers," *Artforum* 12, no. 2 (October 1973): 35.

30 The conceptual and process-based underpinnings of Long's work are exemplified by his decision to assemble a sculpture in its first iteration, but not supervise subsequent installations. Long, like Sol LeWitt, provides a document with basic instructions upon the sale of a work.

31 Ann Goldstein, "Richard Long," in Goldstein and Rorimer, *Reconsidering the Object of Art: 1965–1975*, 169.

32 While Fulton evidently composes his images, his work reflects a concern with photography's conceptual underpinnings and gaps, rather than aesthetics. Moreover, he does not consider himself a photographer and allows others to print his works.

33 Bruce Boice, "Jan Dibbets: The Photograph and the Photographed," *Artforum* 11, no. 8 (April 1973): 45.

34 Nico Israel, "Jan Dibbets: Barbara Gladstone Gallery," *Artforum* 39, no. 8 (April 2001): 136.

35 The Hirshhorn's collection also includes Nauman's *Hand to Mouth*, 1967, a wax cast of the artist's arm, as well as his large-scale installation *South America Triangle*, 1981.

36 Joan Simon, "Breaking the Silence: An Interview with Bruce Nauman, 1988" in *Please Pay Attention Please: Bruce Nauman's Words: Writings and Interviews*, ed. Janet Kraynak (Cambridge: Massachusetts Institute of Technology, 2003), 326.

Plates

OPPOSITE
Joseph Kosuth
American, b. Toledo, Ohio, 1945
Self-Defined, 1965
Neon tubing
3⅛ × 27¼ × 1 inches
Joseph H. Hirshhorn Purchase Fund, 2007
The Panza Collection (07.62)

BELOW
Joseph Kosuth
American, b. Toledo, Ohio, 1945
Box, Cube, Empty, Clear, Glass—a Description, 1965
Glass and vinyl lettering
Each 40 × 40 × 40 inches
Joseph H. Hirshhorn Purchase Fund, 2007
The Panza Collection (07.60)

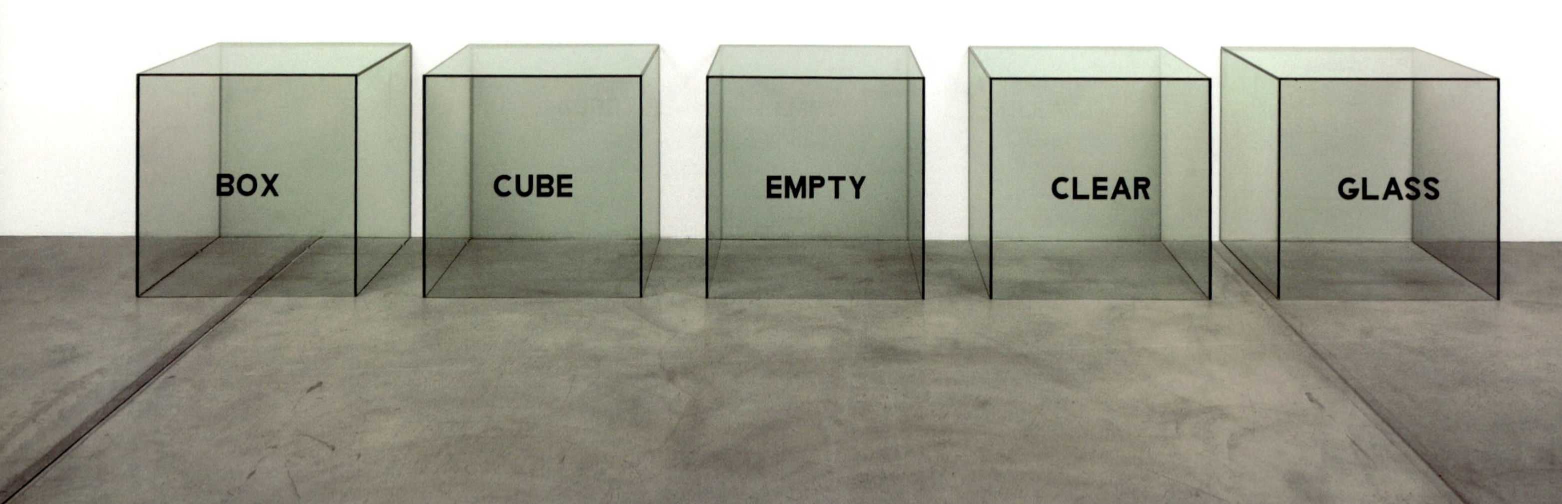

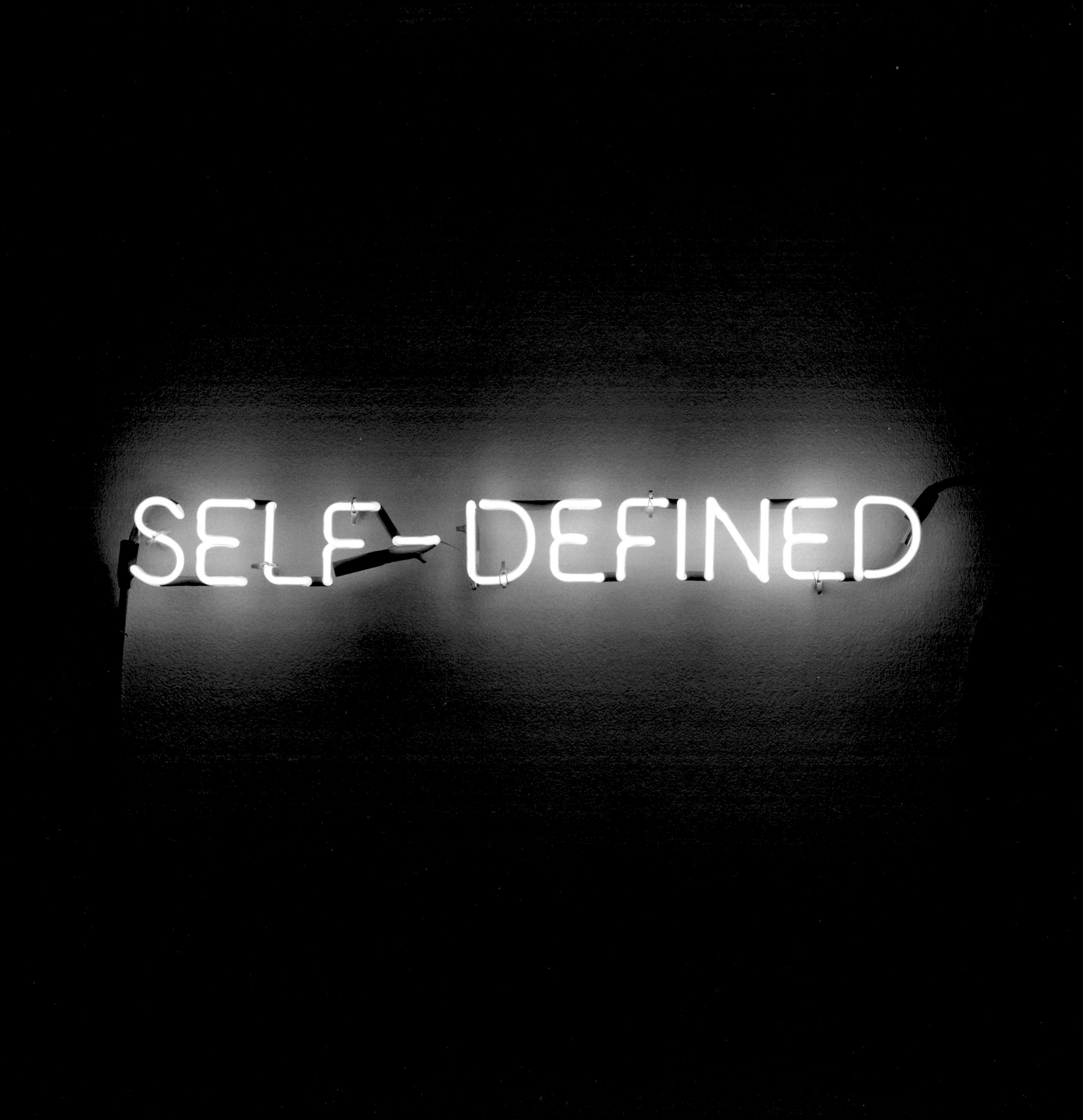

SELF-DEFINED

Joseph Kosuth
American, b. Toledo, Ohio, 1945
'One and Five (Clock) [Eng.-Ita.]', 1965
Gelatin silver prints and wall clock
Each panel 19 × 19 × ½ inches;
clock diameter 12 inches
Joseph H. Hirshhorn Purchase Fund, 2007
The Panza Collection (07.61)

OPPOSITE
Detail

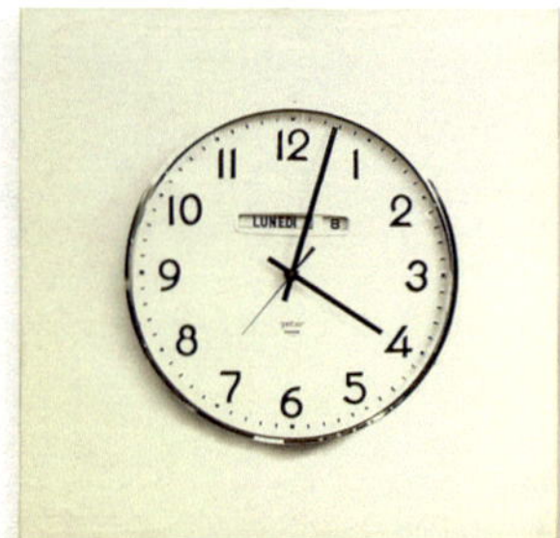

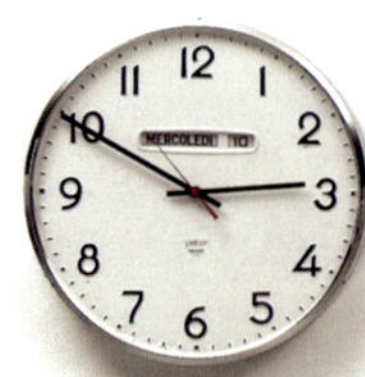

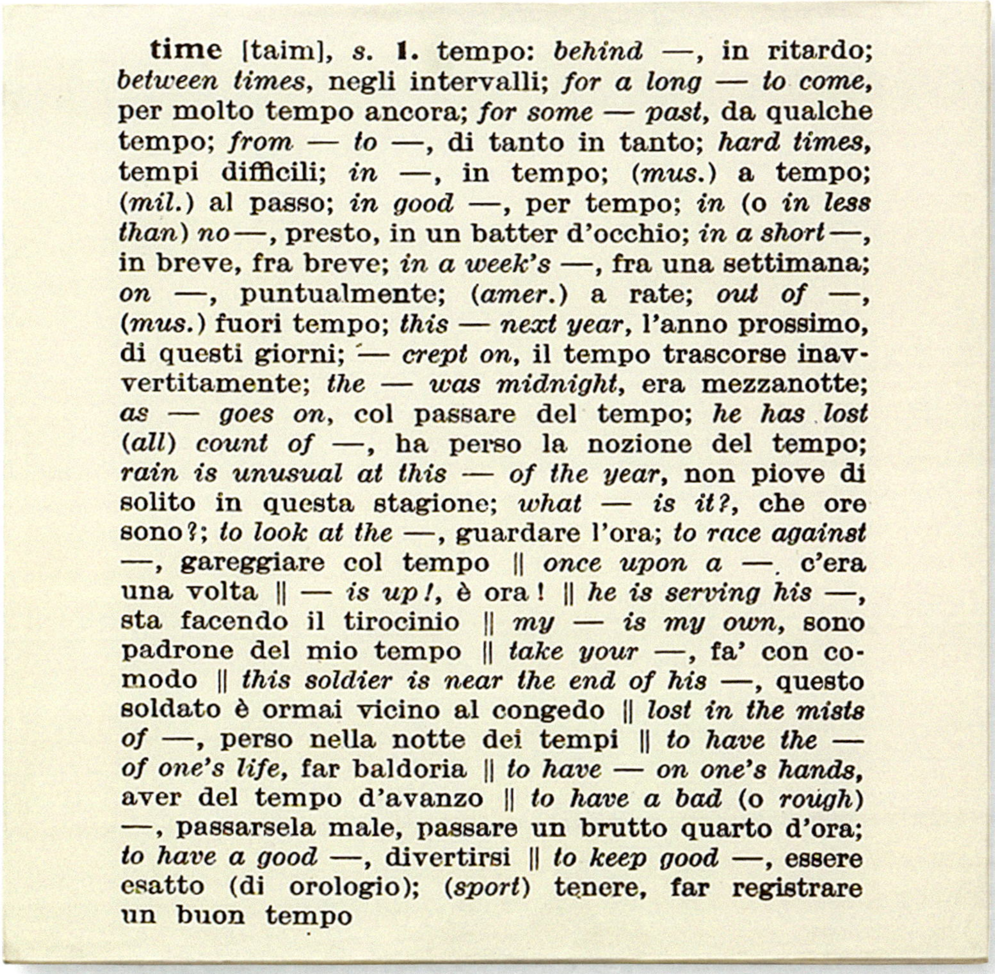

time [taim], *s.* **1.** tempo: *behind* —, in ritardo; *between times*, negli intervalli; *for a long — to come*, per molto tempo ancora; *for some — past*, da qualche tempo; *from — to* —, di tanto in tanto; *hard times*, tempi difficili; *in* —, in tempo; (*mus.*) a tempo; (*mil.*) al passo; *in good* —, per tempo; *in* (o *in less than*) *no* —, presto, in un batter d'occhio; *in a short* —, in breve, fra breve; *in a week's* —, fra una settimana; *on* —, puntualmente; (*amer.*) a rate; *out of* —, (*mus.*) fuori tempo; *this — next year*, l'anno prossimo, di questi giorni; *— crept on*, il tempo trascorse inavvertitamente; *the — was midnight*, era mezzanotte; *as — goes on*, col passare del tempo; *he has lost* (*all*) *count of* —, ha perso la nozione del tempo; *rain is unusual at this — of the year*, non piove di solito in questa stagione; *what — is it?*, che ore sono?; *to look at the* —, guardare l'ora; *to race against* —, gareggiare col tempo || *once upon a* —, c'era una volta || *— is up!*, è ora! || *he is serving his* —, sta facendo il tirocinio || *my — is my own*, sono padrone del mio tempo || *take your* —, fa' con comodo || *this soldier is near the end of his* —, questo soldato è ormai vicino al congedo || *lost in the mists of* —, perso nella notte dei tempi || *to have the — of one's life*, far baldoria || *to have — on one's hands*, aver del tempo d'avanzo || *to have a bad* (o *rough*) —, passarsela male, passare un brutto quarto d'ora; *to have a good* —, divertirsi || *to keep good* —, essere esatto (di orologio); (*sport*) tenere, far registrare un buon tempo

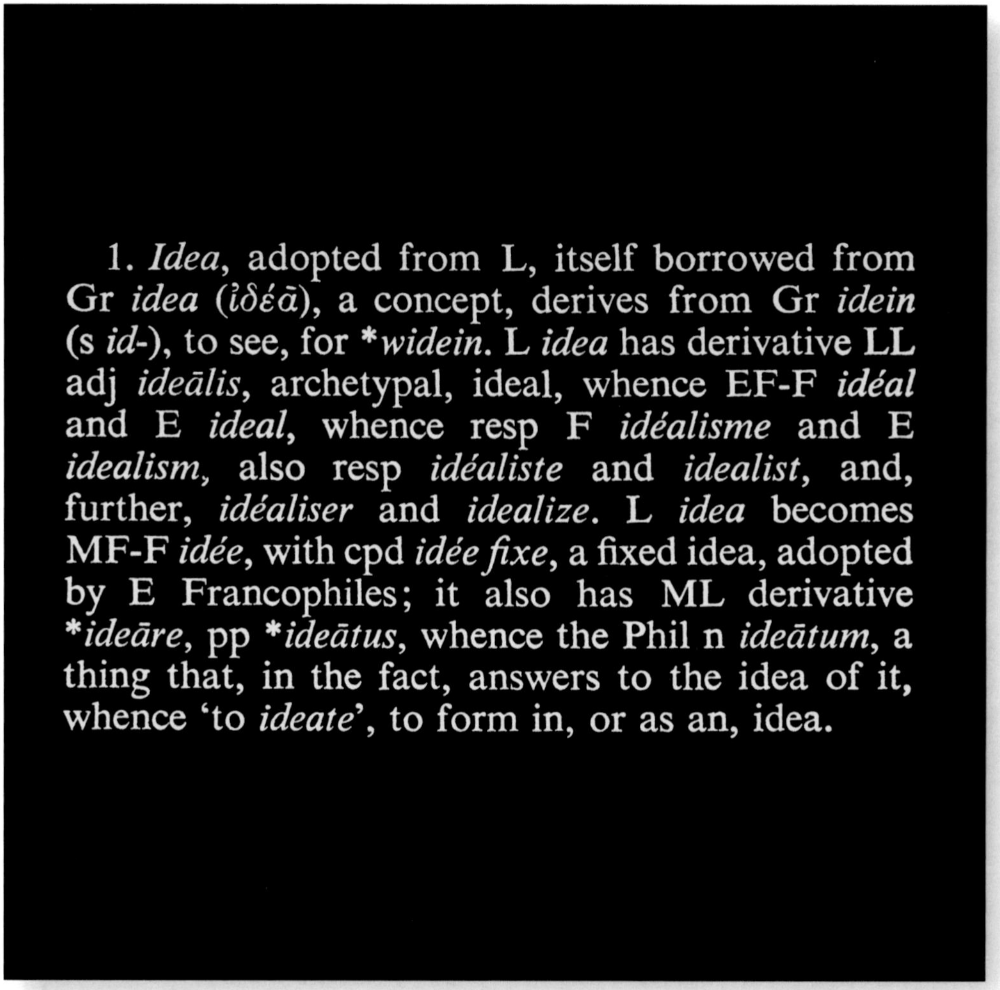

1. *Idea*, adopted from L, itself borrowed from Gr *idea* (*ἰδέᾱ*), a concept, derives from Gr *idein* (s *id-*), to see, for **widein*. L *idea* has derivative LL adj *ideālis*, archetypal, ideal, whence EF-F *idéal* and E *ideal*, whence resp F *idéalisme* and E *idealism*, also resp *idéaliste* and *idealist*, and, further, *idéaliser* and *idealize*. L *idea* becomes MF-F *idée*, with cpd *idée fixe*, a fixed idea, adopted by E Francophiles; it also has ML derivative **ideāre*, pp **ideātus*, whence the Phil n *ideātum*, a thing that, in the fact, answers to the idea of it, whence 'to *ideate*', to form in, or as an, idea.

Joseph Kosuth
American, b. Toledo, Ohio, 1945
'Titled (Art as Idea as Idea) [idea]', 1966
C-print on paper on plastic panel
60 × 60 × ¼ inches
Joseph H. Hirshhorn Purchase Fund, 2007
The Panza Collection (07.63)

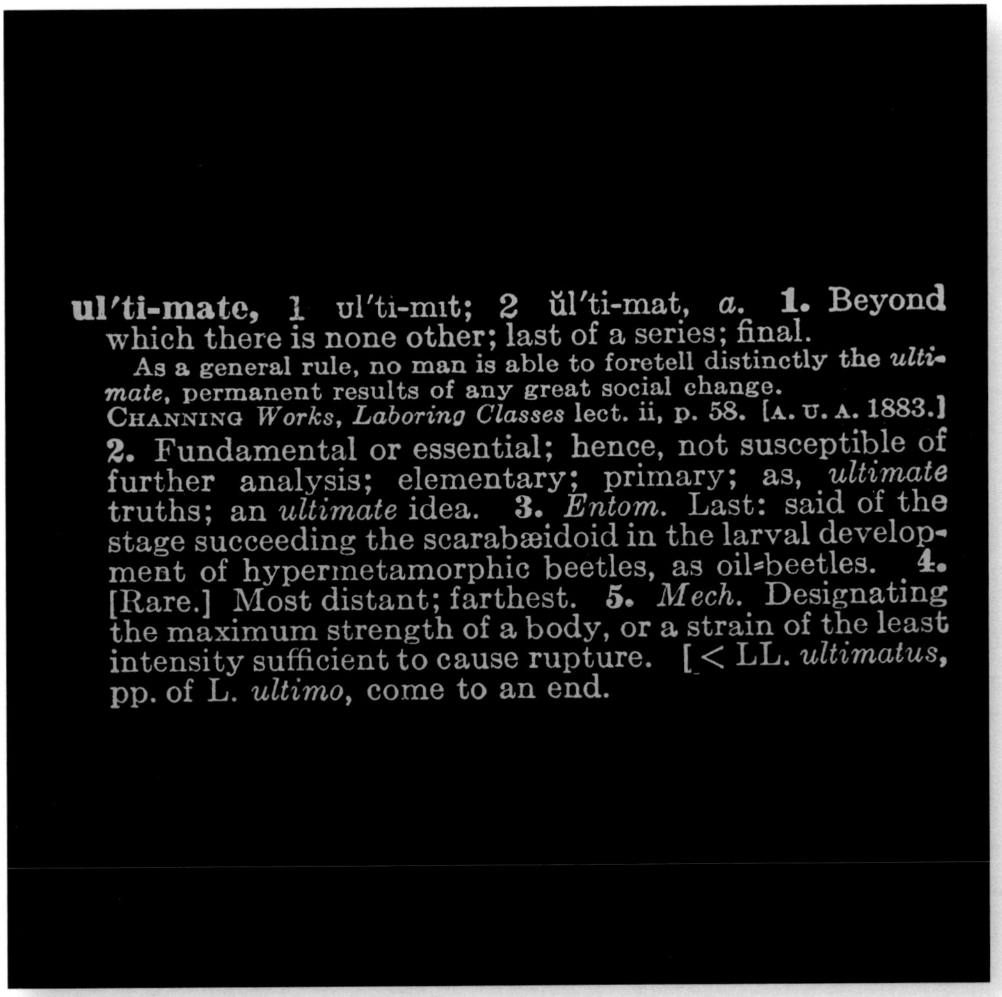

ul′ti-mate, 1 ul′ti-mit; 2 ŭl′ti-mat, *a.* **1.** Beyond which there is none other; last of a series; final.

As a general rule, no man is able to foretell distinctly the *ultimate*, permanent results of any great social change.
CHANNING *Works, Laboring Classes* lect. ii, p. 58. [A. U. A. 1883.]

2. Fundamental or essential; hence, not susceptible of further analysis; elementary; primary; as, *ultimate* truths; an *ultimate* idea. **3.** *Entom.* Last: said of the stage succeeding the scarabæidoid in the larval development of hypermetamorphic beetles, as oil-beetles. **4.** [Rare.] Most distant; farthest. **5.** *Mech.* Designating the maximum strength of a body, or a strain of the least intensity sufficient to cause rupture. [< LL. *ultimatus*, pp. of L. *ultimo*, come to an end.

Joseph Kosuth
American, b. Toledo, Ohio, 1945
'Titled (Art as Idea as Idea) [ultimate]', 1967
C-print on paper on plastic panel
60 × 60 × ¼ inches
Joseph H. Hirshhorn Purchase Fund, 2007
The Panza Collection (07.64)

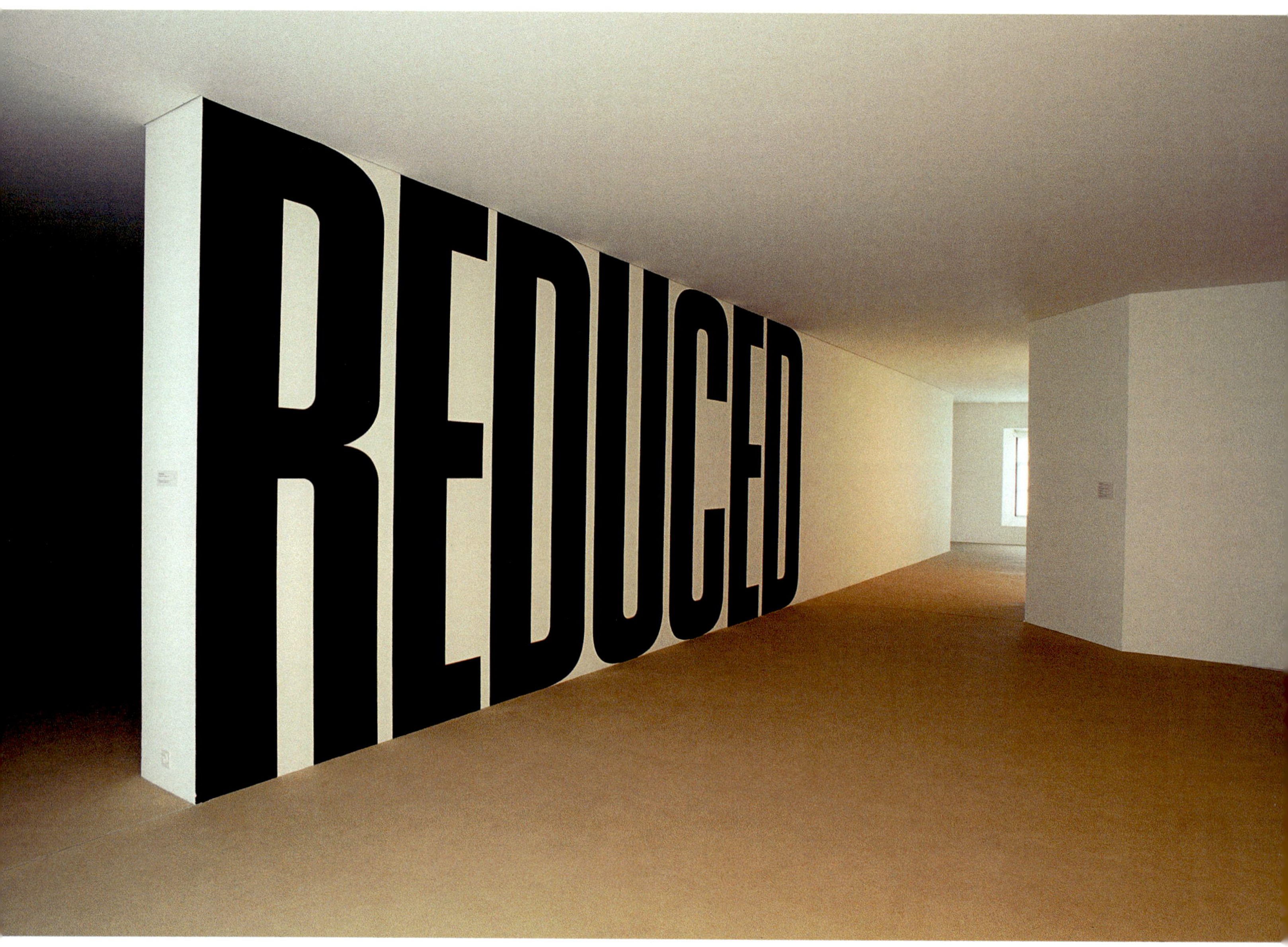

Lawrence Weiner
American, b. New York, New York, 1940
REDUCED, Cat. No. 102, 1970
Paint on wall
Dimensions variable
Joseph H. Hirshhorn Purchase Fund, 2007
The Panza Collection (07.73)

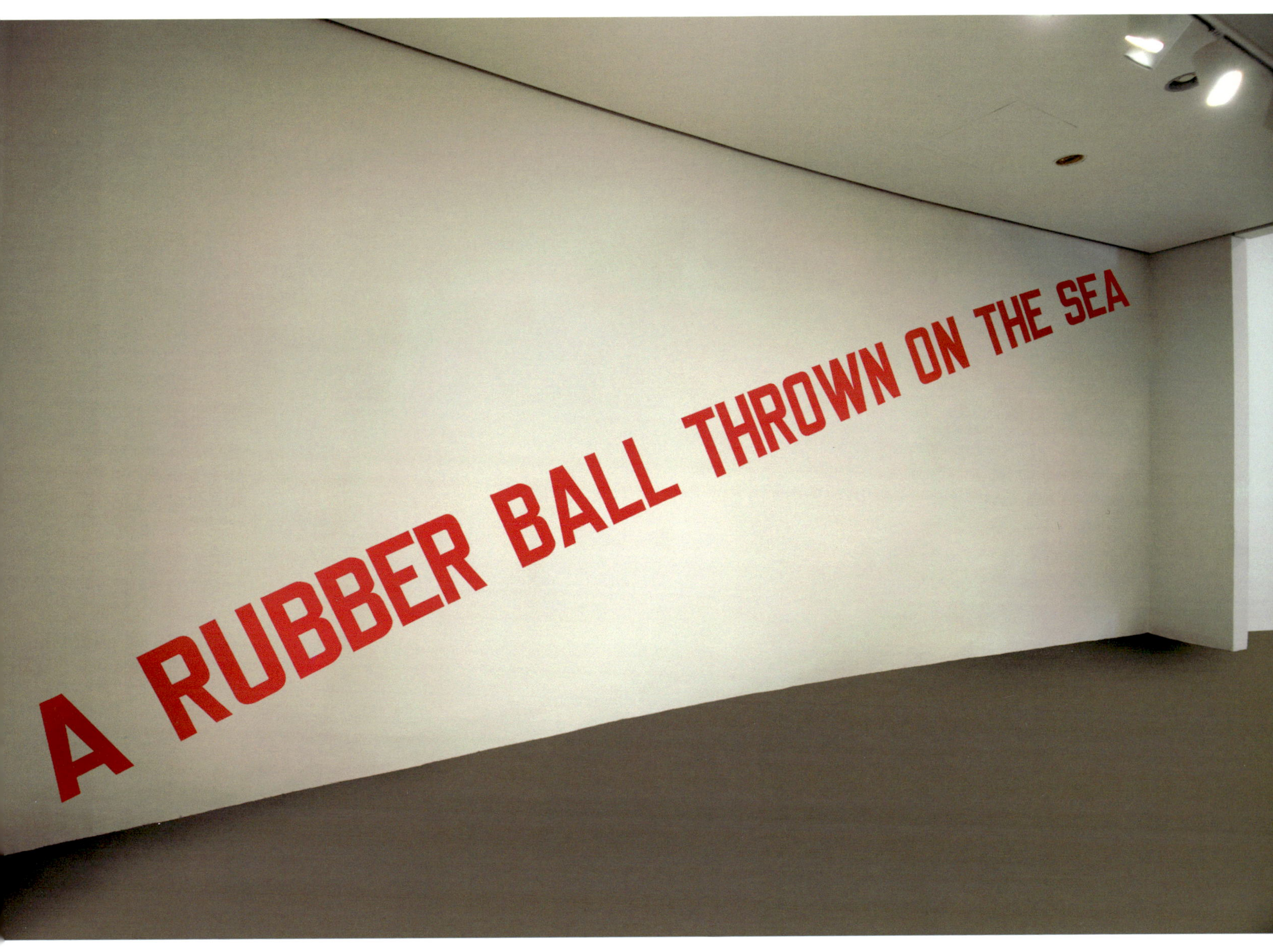

Lawrence Weiner
American, b. New York, New York, 1940
Installation plan of *A rubber ball thrown on the sea, Cat. No. 146*, 1969
Vinyl lettering on wall
Dimensions variable
Joseph H. Hirshhorn Purchase Fund, 2007
The Panza Collection (07.72)

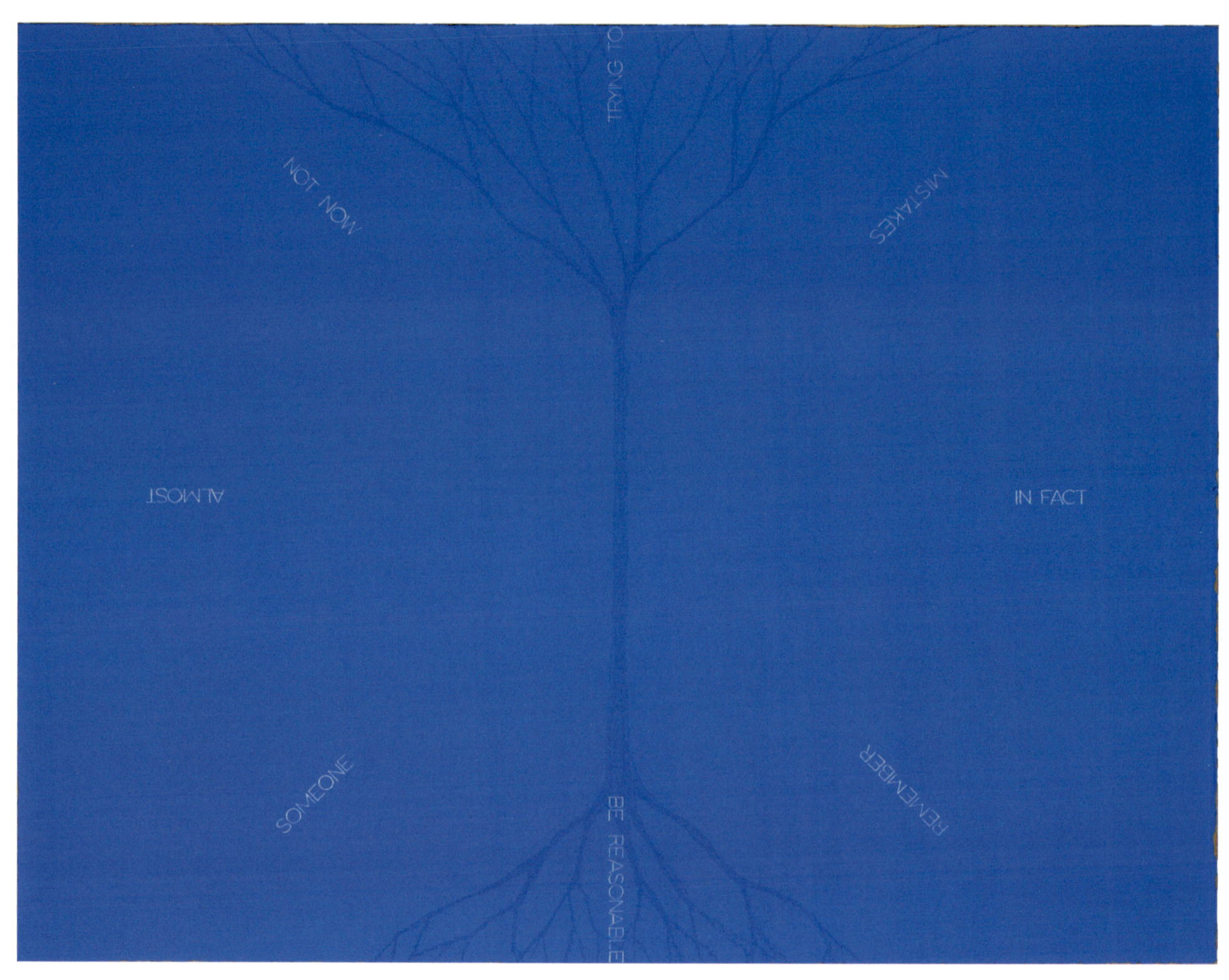

Robert Barry
American, b. New York, New York, 1936
Sketch and instructions (on verso) for *Untitled*, 1983
Paint, oil stick, and vinyl lettering on wall
Dimensions variable
Joseph H. Hirshhorn Purchase Fund, 2007
The Panza Collection (07.39)

↑
TOP

PLAN FOR: UNTITLED. 1983

WALLPIECE FIRST INSTALLED AT LEO CASTELLI GALLERY 1983. SEE PHOTOS.

① WALL PAINTED BLUE (ORIGINAL INSTALLATION BENJAMIN MOORE SPECTRA BLUE BT-67 SATIN FINISH ENAMEL WAS USED)

② 'TREE' IMAGE WAS DRAWN WITH RED PENCIL SO THAT BRANCHES + ROOTS APPEAR TO GO BEYOND END OF WALL AT CEILING AND FLOOR (RED FELT TIP PEN MAY ALSO BE USED).

③ SECOND COAT OF BLUE PAINT IS CAREFULLY ROLLED OVER 'TREE' SO THAT ONLY FAINT IMAGE APPEARS THROUGH PAINT. THIRD COAT OR TOUCHUP MAY BE NEEDED. FLAT LATEX PAINT.

④ WORDS ARE APPLIED SO THAT TOP + BOTTOM WORDS (TRYING TO + BE REASONABLE) ARE ABOUT 1" FROM CEILING + FLOOR. THIS DETERMINES SIZE OF CIRCUMFERENCE. SOFT SILVER CRAYON WAS USED, BUT GLOSSY SILVER ENAMEL MAY ALSO BE USED FOR MORE PERMANENT INSTALLATION.

ALL DIMENSIONS ARE VARIABLE. GENERAL PROPORTIONS MUST BE KEPT.

WHENEVER POSSIBLE THE ARTIST SHOULD BE CONSULTED WHENEVER THE PIECE IS REINSTALLED.

ROBERT BARRY

LETTERS WERE 2" HIGH IN ORIGINAL INSTALLATION

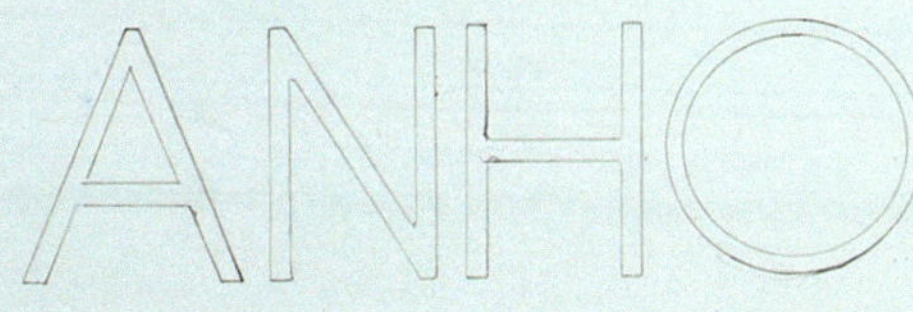

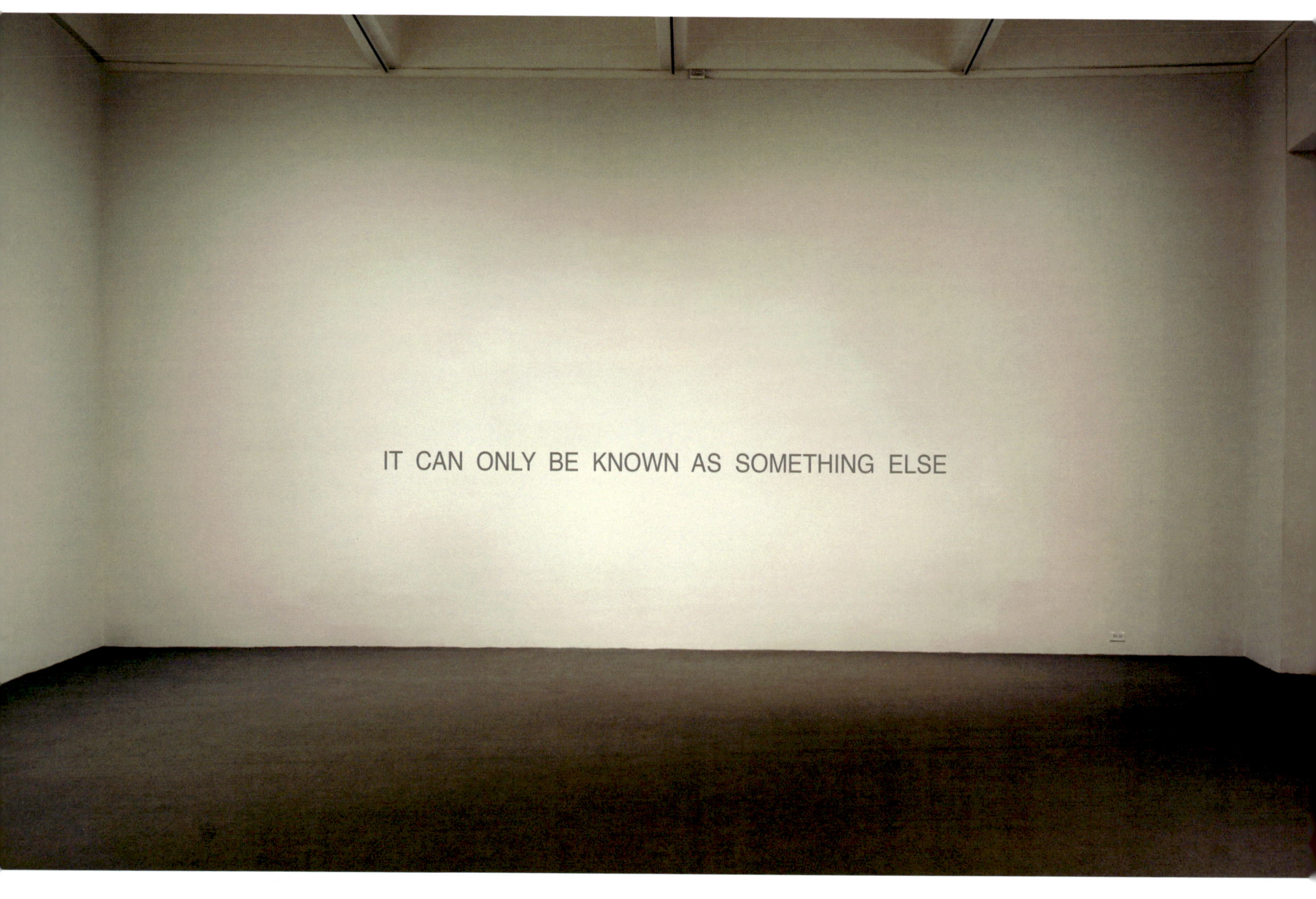
IT CAN ONLY BE KNOWN AS SOMETHING ELSE

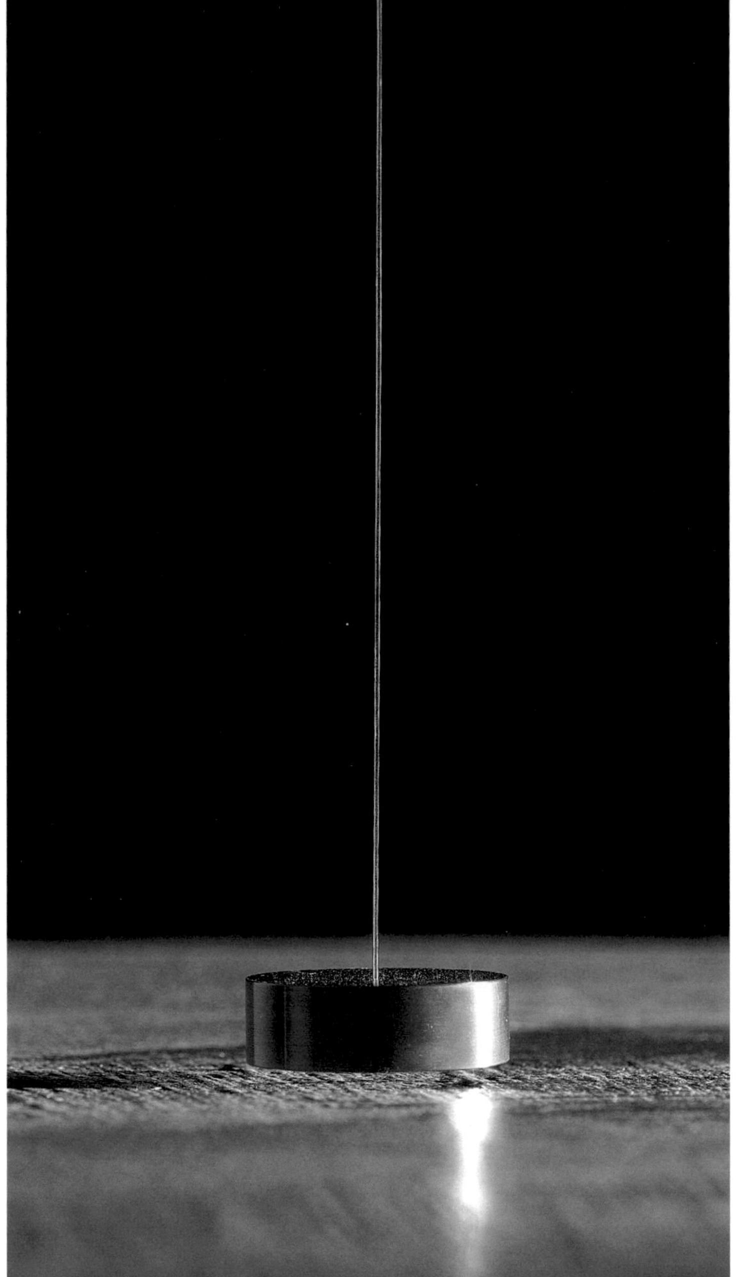

OPPOSITE
Robert Barry
American, b. New York, New York, 1936
Installation plan for *It Can Only Be Known as Something Else*, 1969
Vinyl lettering on wall
Dimensions variable
Joseph H. Hirshhorn Purchase Fund, 2007
The Panza Collection (07.37)

LEFT
Robert Barry
American, b. New York, New York, 1936
Steel Disc Suspended 1/8 in. Above Floor, 1967
Steel and nylon string
Dimensions variable;
disc 2 inches diameter × 5/8 inches high
Joseph H. Hirshhorn Purchase Fund, 2007
The Panza Collection (07.36)

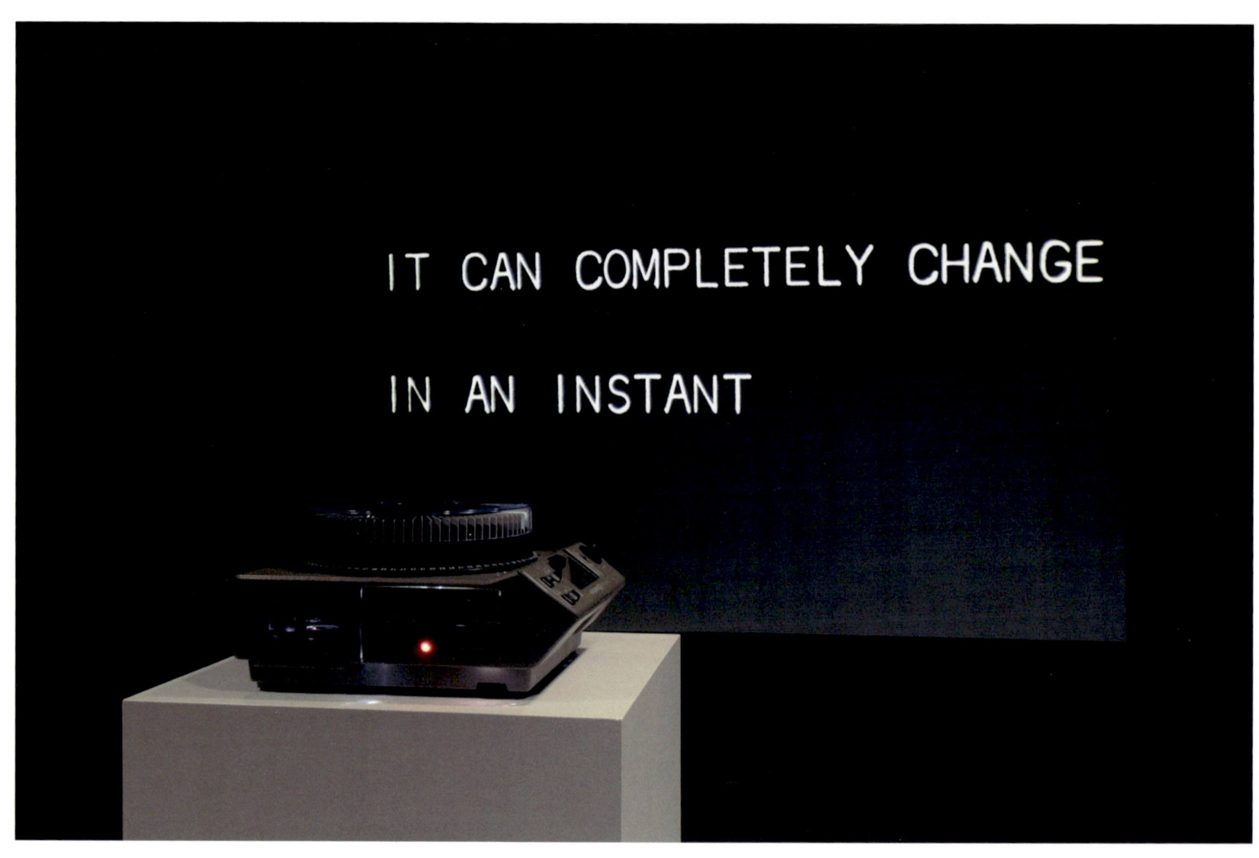

Robert Barry
American, b. New York, New York, 1936
It..., 1969–71
35mm slides (59 with text, 1 blank) and projector
Dimensions variable
Joseph H. Hirshhorn Purchase Fund, 2007
The Panza Collection (07.38)

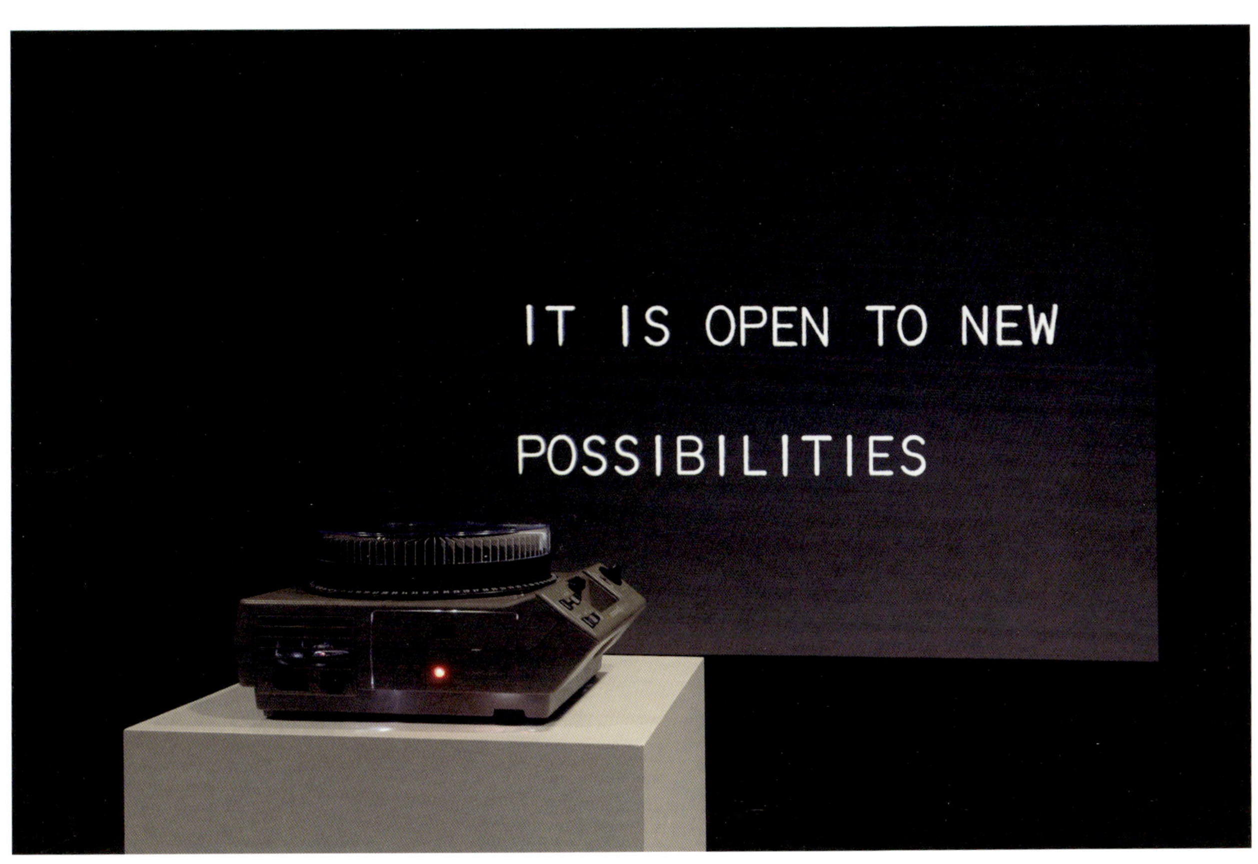
IT IS OPEN TO NEW
POSSIBILITIES

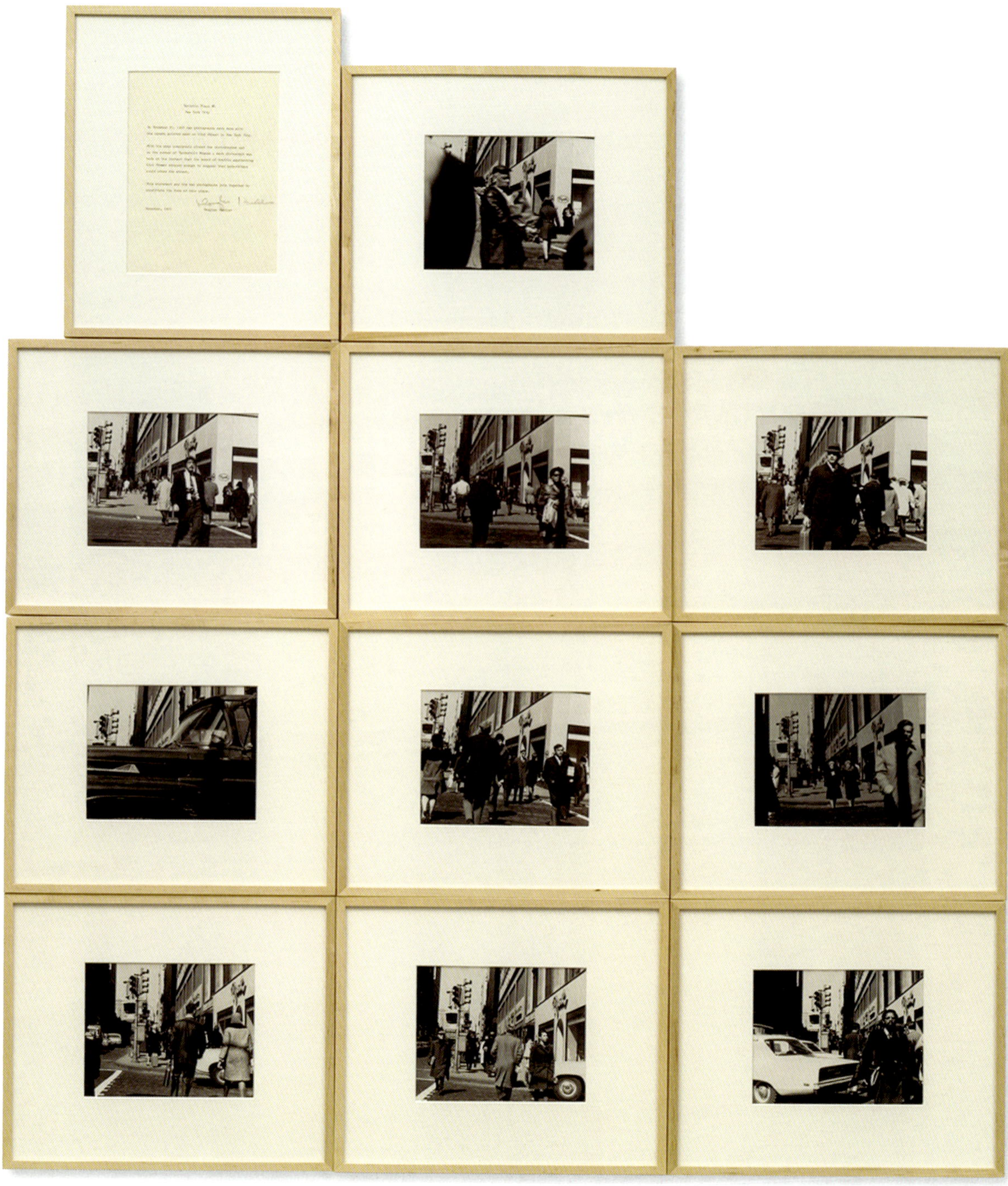

Variable Piece #4

New York City

On November 23, 1968 ten photographs were made with the camera pointed west on 42nd Street in New York City.

With his eyes completely closed the photographer sat on the corner of Vanderbilt Avenue ; each photograph was made at the instant that the sound of traffic approaching 42nd Street stopped enough to suggest that pedestrians could cross the street.

This statement and the ten photographs join together to constitute the form of this piece.

November, 1968 Douglas Huebler

OPPOSITE

Douglas Huebler

American, b. Ann Arbor, Michigan, 1924–1997

Variable Piece #4 New York City, 1968

Gelatin silver prints and ink on paper

Each print 12½ × 14¼ inches;

statement 15¾ × 13⅜ inches

Joseph H. Hirshhorn Purchase Fund, 2007

The Panza Collection (07.50)

LEFT

Detail

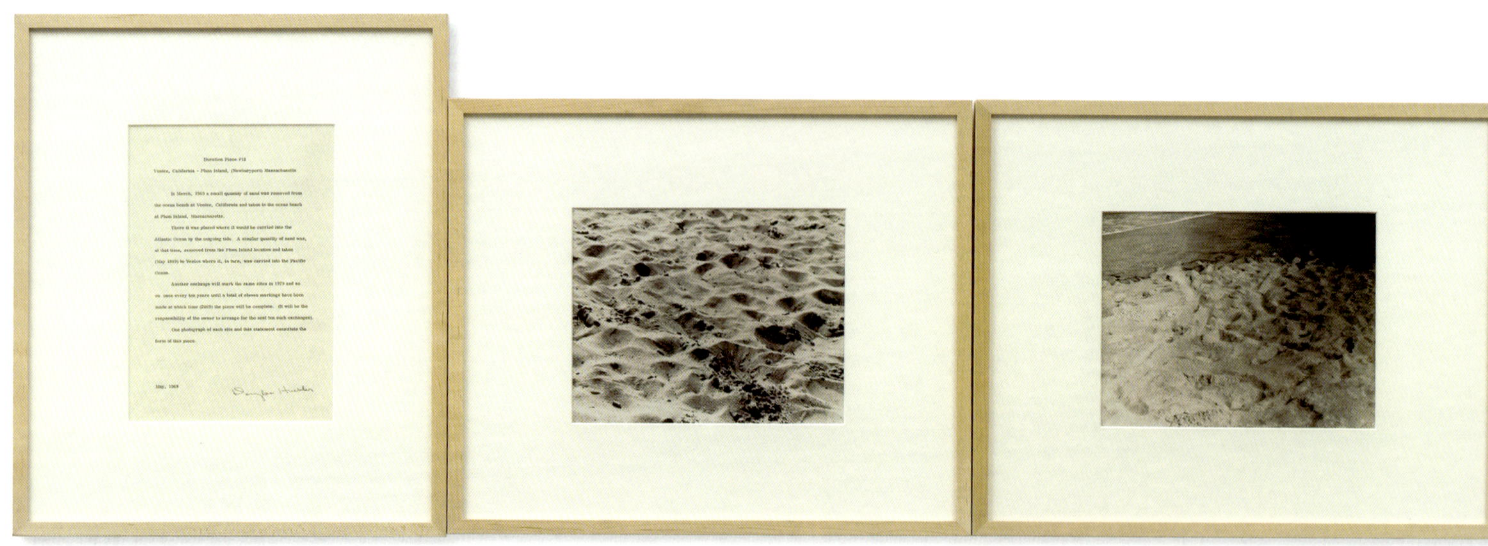

ABOVE
Douglas Huebler
American, b. Ann Arbor, Michigan, 1924–1997
Duration Piece #12 Venice, California–Plum Island (Newbury Port), Massachusetts, 1969
Gelatin silver prints and ink on paper
Each print: 14⅛ × 12¼ inches;
statement 15¾ × 13⅜ inches
Joseph H. Hirshhorn Purchase Fund, 2007
The Panza Collection (07.51)

OPPOSITE
Detail

Duration Piece #12

Venice, California - Plum Island, (Newburyport) Massachusetts

In March, 1969 a small quantity of sand was removed from the ocean beach at Venice, California and taken to the ocean beach at Plum Island, Massachusetts.

There it was placed where it would be carried into the Atlantic Ocean by the outgoing tide. A similar quantity of sand was, at that time, removed from the Plum Island location and taken (May 1969) to Venice where it, in turn, was carried into the Pacific Ocean.

Another exchange will mark the same sites in 1979 and so on: once every ten years until a total of eleven markings have been made at which time (2069) the piece will be complete. (It will be the responsibility of the owner to arrange for the next ten such exchanges).

One photograph of each site and this statement constitute the form of this piece.

May, 1969

Douglas Huebler

Douglas Huebler
American, b. Ann Arbor, Michigan, 1924–1997
Drawing (Reflecting Essence), 1970
Ink on paper
$14\frac{1}{8} \times 12\frac{3}{8}$ inches
Joseph H. Hirshhorn Purchase Fund, 2007
The Panza Collection (07.52)

CETTE SURFACE REFLÈTE À CET INSTANT MÊME LE CHANGEMENT IMPERCEPTIBLE DE L'ESSENCE PHYSIQUE DE L'OBSERVATEUR.
THIS SURFACE IS, AT THIS INSTANT, REFLECTING THE IMPERCEPTIBLY CHANGING PHYSICAL ESSENCE OF ITS PERCIPIENT.
1970

BELOW
Sol LeWitt
American, b. Hartford, Connecticut, 1928–2007
Certificate and instructions for
Wall Drawing #3, 1969
Graphite on wall
Dimensions variable
Joseph H. Hirshhorn Purchase Fund, 2007
The Panza Collection (07.65)

OPPOSITE
Original installation of the work at Konrad Fischer gallery, Neubrückstraße, Dusseldorf

CERTIFICATE

This is to certify that the Sol LeWitt wall drawing number 3 evidenced by this certificate is authentic.

A 40" (100 cm) band of vertical and both sets of diagonal lines superimposed, centered top to bottom, running the length of the wall.

Black pencil
First Drawn by: Hans Hermann and others
First Installation: Konrad Fischer, Dusseldorf, Germany
April, 1969

This certification is the signature for the wall drawing and must accompany the wall drawing if it is sold or otherwise transferred.

Certified by Sol LeWitt
Sol LeWitt

© Copyright Sol LeWitt
Date

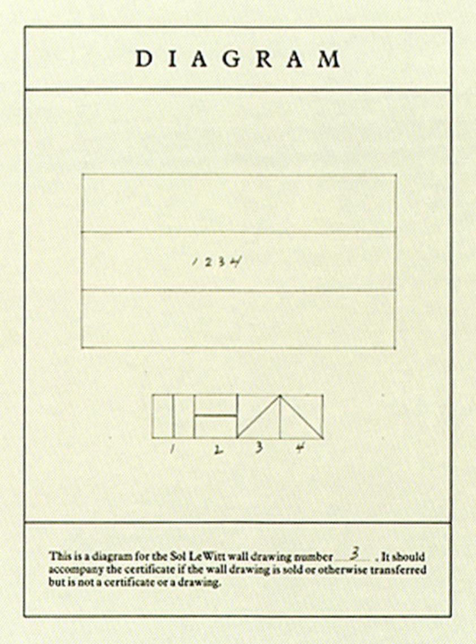
DIAGRAM

1 2 3 4

1 2 3 4

This is a diagram for the Sol LeWitt wall drawing number 3. It should accompany the certificate if the wall drawing is sold or otherwise transferred but is not a certificate or a drawing.

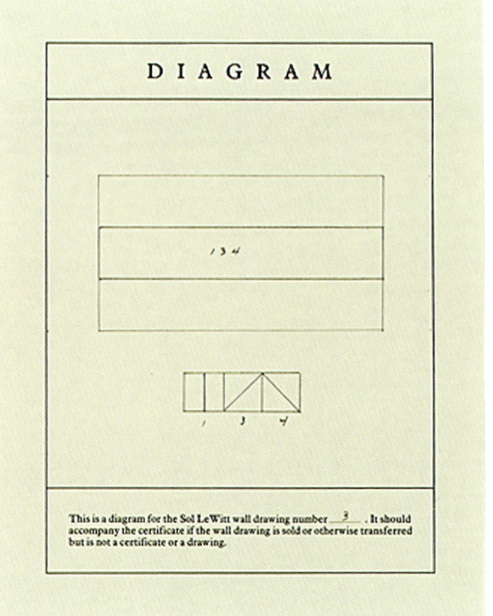
DIAGRAM

1 3 4

1 3 4

This is a diagram for the Sol LeWitt wall drawing number 3. It should accompany the certificate if the wall drawing is sold or otherwise transferred but is not a certificate or a drawing.

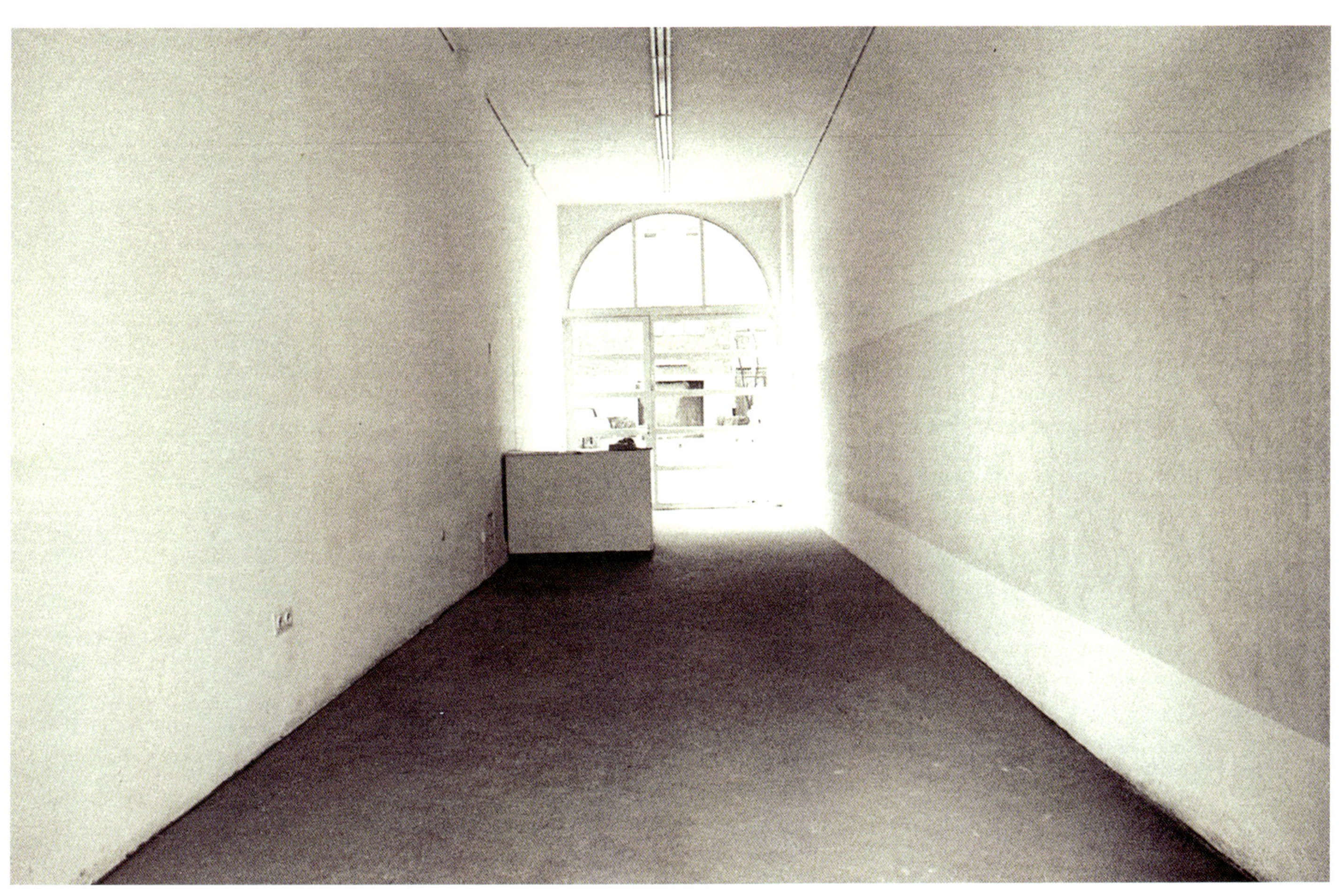

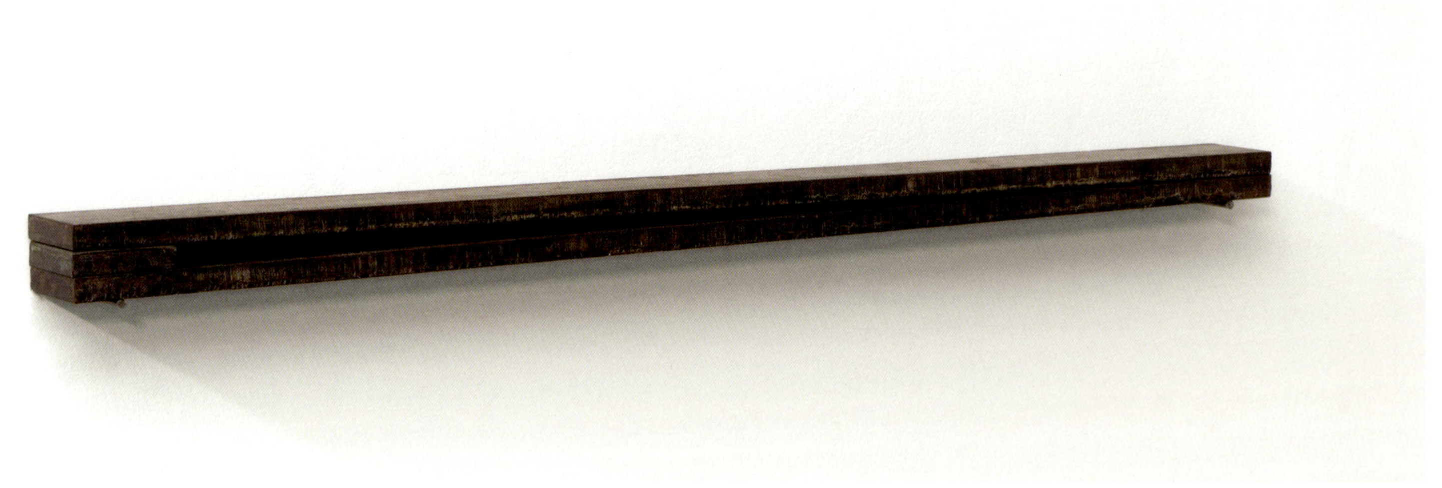

ABOVE
Richard Nonas
American, b. New York, New York, 1936
Genoa Slot Series (1 Down 1 Up), 1974
Steel
2⅛ × 39½ × 3 inches
Joseph H. Hirshhorn Purchase Fund, 2007
The Panza Collection (07.68)

RIGHT
Richard Nonas
American, b. New York, New York, 1936
Bari Shortline, 1975
Wood
12⅝ × 101⅛ × 8 inches
Joseph H. Hirshhorn Purchase Fund, 2007
The Panza Collection (07.70)

OPPOSITE
Richard Nonas
American, b. New York, New York, 1936
Salita Nord #2 (Fault Line), 1974
Steel
1½ × 44½ × 78¾ inches
Joseph H. Hirshhorn Purchase Fund, 2007
The Panza Collection (07.69)

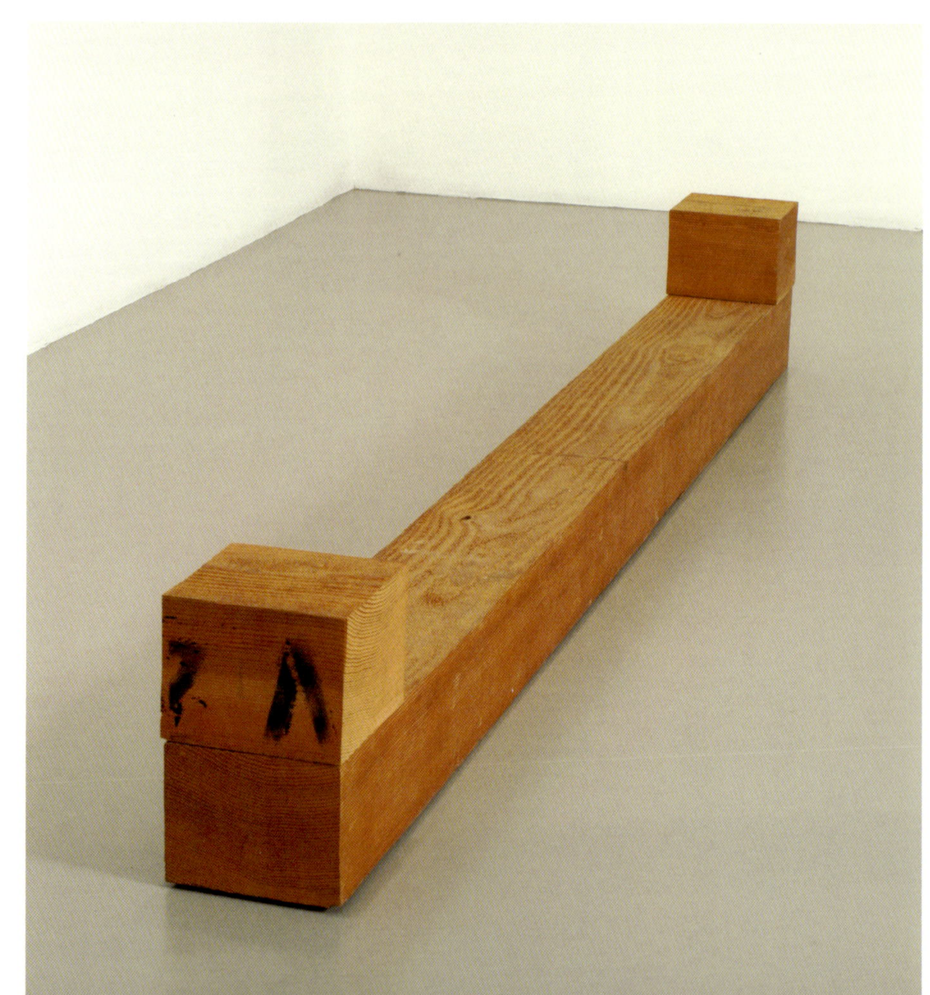

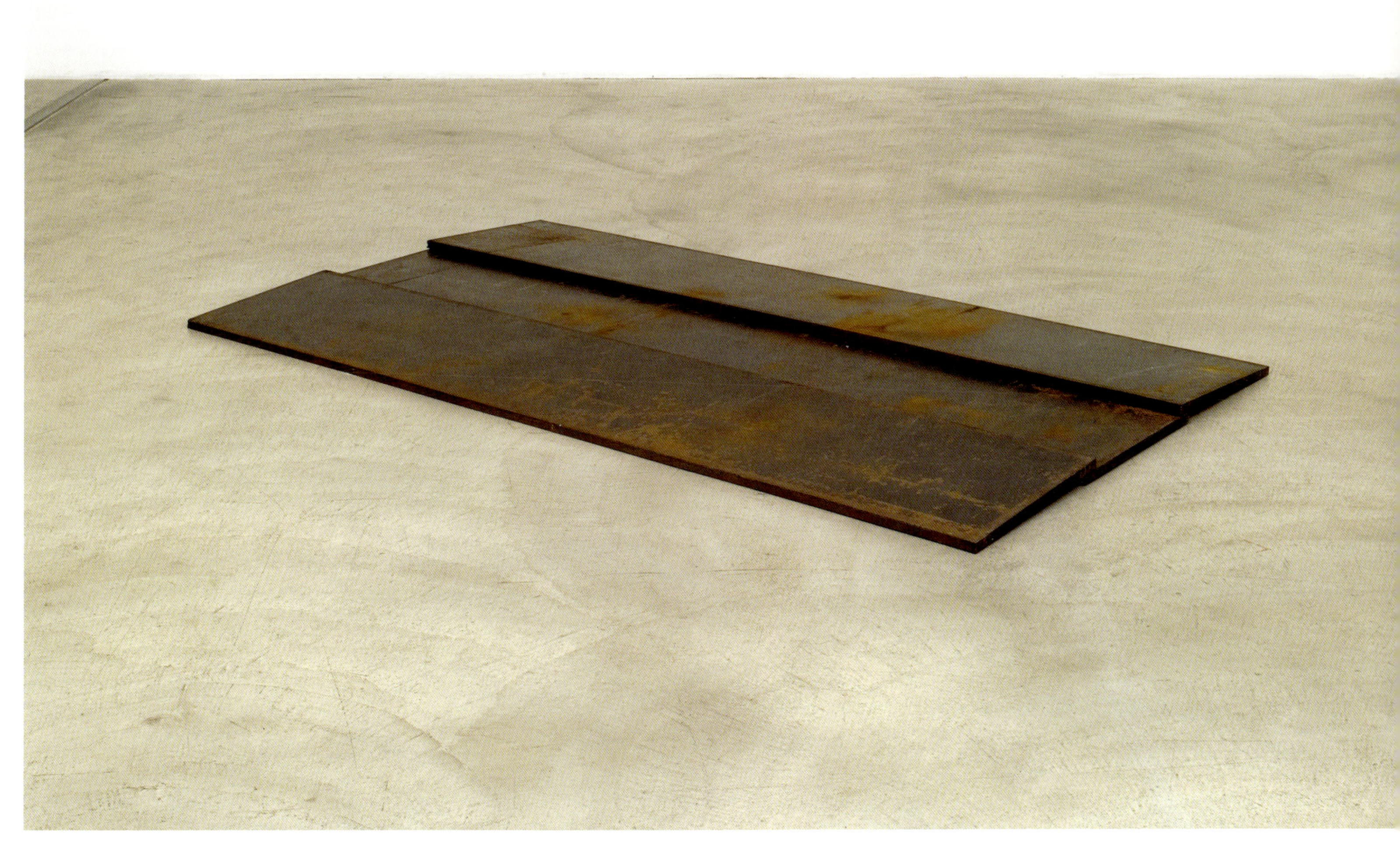

ABOVE
Robert Irwin
American, b. Long Beach, California, 1928
Untitled, 1963–65
Acrylic paint on canvas on panel
82⅜ × 84½ inches
Joseph H. Hirshhorn Purchase Fund, 2007
The Panza Collection (07.53)

OPPOSITE
Enlarged detail

RIGHT
Robert Irwin
American, b. Long Beach, California, 1928
Untitled, 1970–71
Acrylic
142½ × 8½ × 8½ inches
Joseph H. Hirshhorn Purchase Fund, 2007
The Panza Collection (07.55)

OPPOSITE
Robert Irwin
American, b. Long Beach, California, 1928
Untitled, 1966–67
Aluminum, acrylic paint, and lamps
Disc diameter 60 inches
Joseph H. Hirshhorn Purchase Fund, 2007
The Panza Collection (07.54)

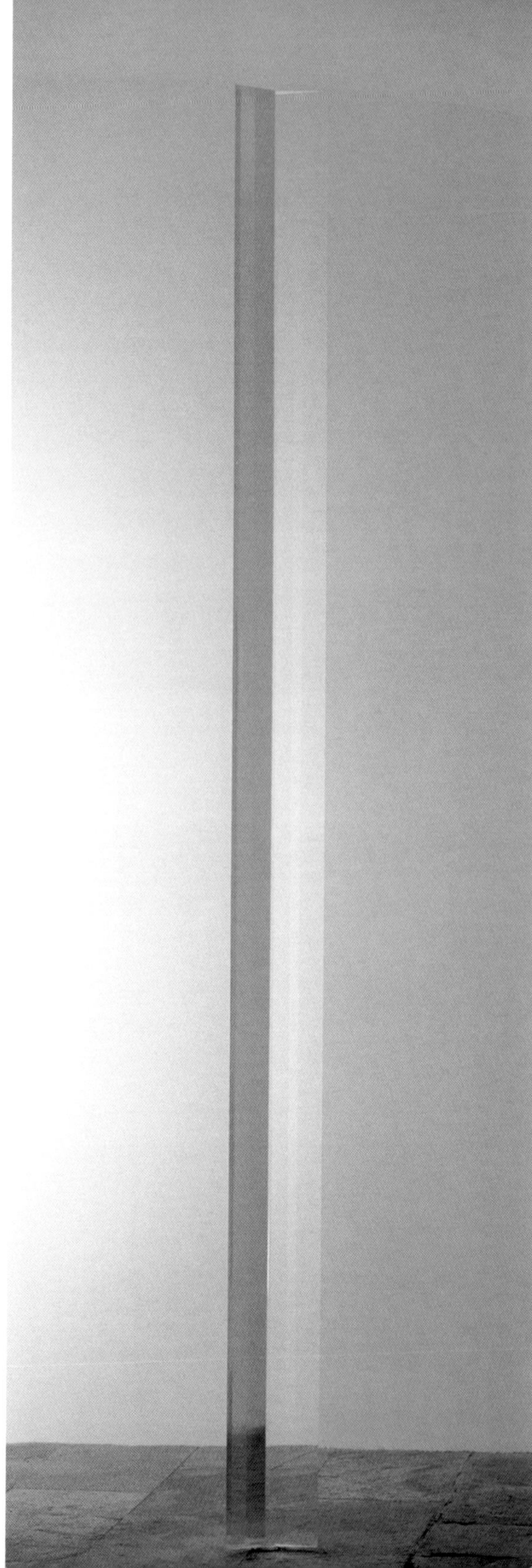

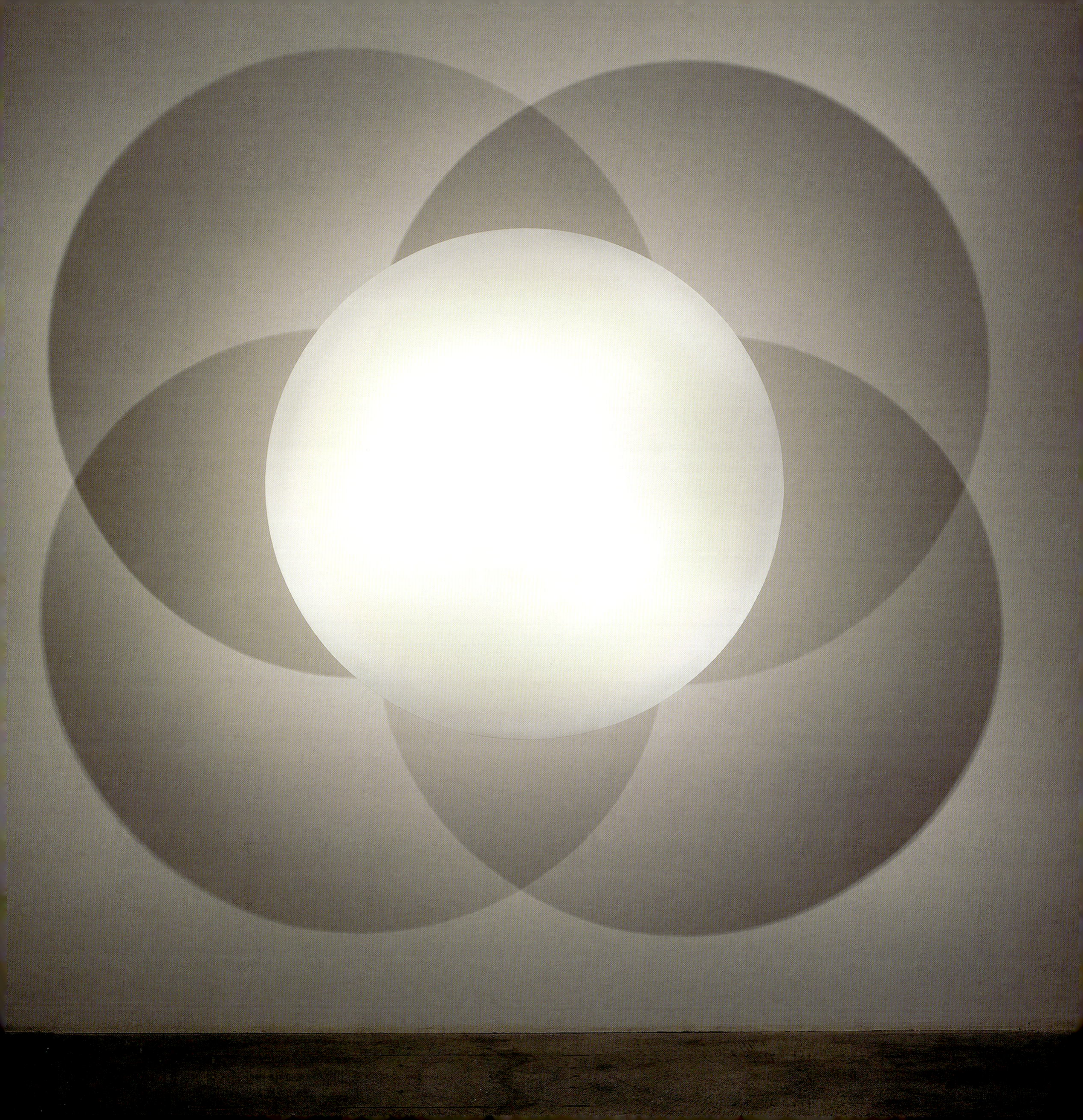

Doug Wheeler
American, b. Globe, Arizona, 1939
Eindhoven, Environmental Light Installation, 1969
Neon tubing
144 × 192 inches
Joseph H. Hirshhorn Purchase Fund, 2007
The Panza Collection (07.74)

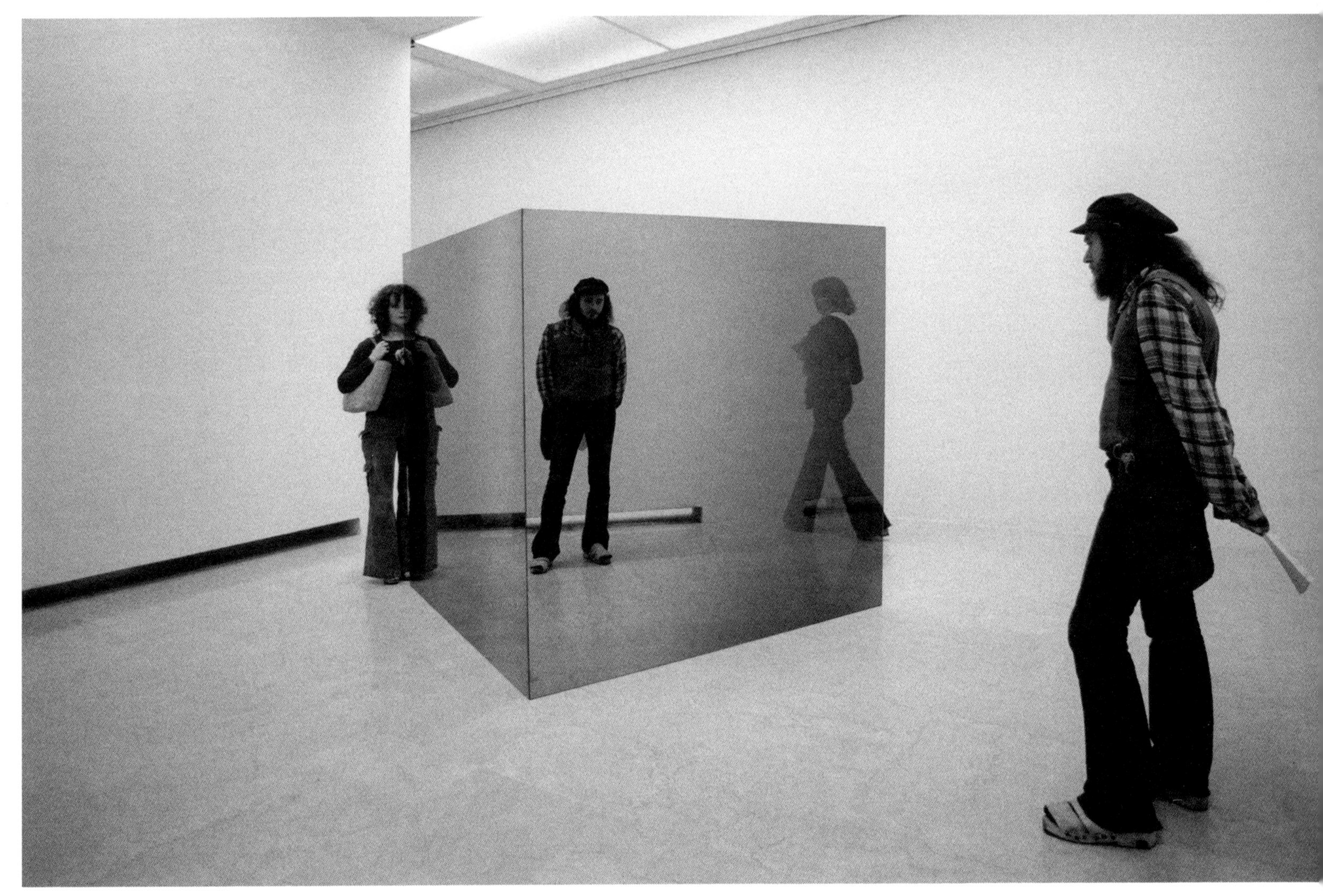

Larry Bell
American, b. Chicago, Illinois, 1939
Untitled, 1973
Vacuum-plated glass
Each panel 72 × 72 × 3/8 inches
Joseph H. Hirshhorn Purchase Fund, 2007
The Panza Collection (07.40)

On Kawara, Roman Opalka, Hanne Darboven

OPPOSITE AND FOLLOWING PAGES

On Kawara
Japanese, b. Kariya, 1933
Detail of *Oct. 24, 1971*, 1971
Cardboard box, newspaper,
and acrylic paint on canvas
10¾ × 13½ × 1⅞ inches
Joseph H. Hirshhorn Purchase Fund, 2007
The Panza Collection (07.57)

On Kawara
Japanese, b. Kariya, 1933
Oct. 26, 1971, 1971
Cardboard box, newspaper,
and acrylic paint on canvas
10¾ × 13½ × 1⅞ inches
Joseph H. Hirshhorn Purchase Fund, 2007
The Panza Collection (07.58)

On Kawara
Japanese, b. Kariya, 1933
Oct. 29, 1971, 1971
Cardboard box, newspaper, and acrylic
paint on canvas
8½ × 10½ × 1⅞ inches
Joseph H. Hirshhorn Purchase Fund, 2007
The Panza Collection (07.59)

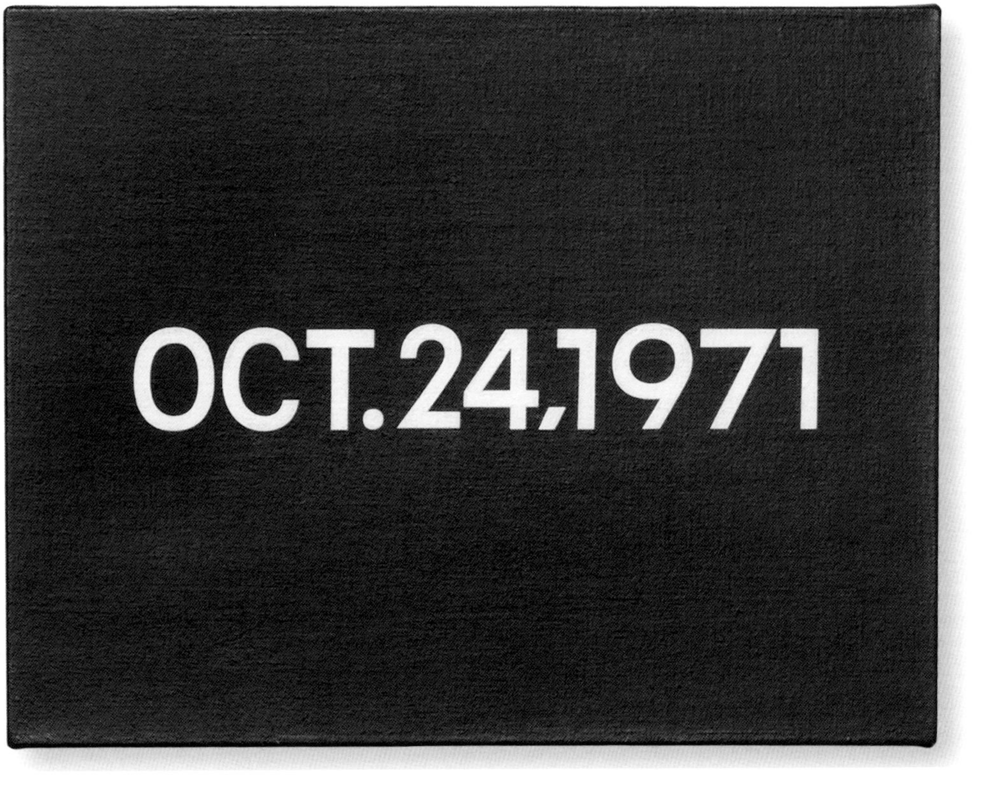

OCT.24,1971

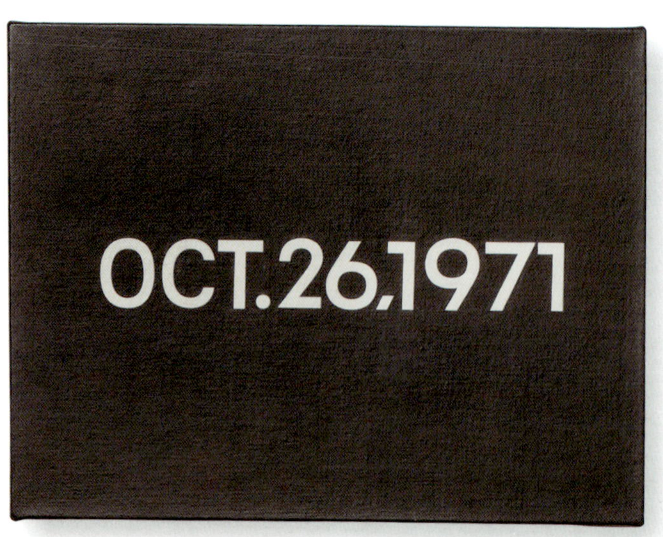

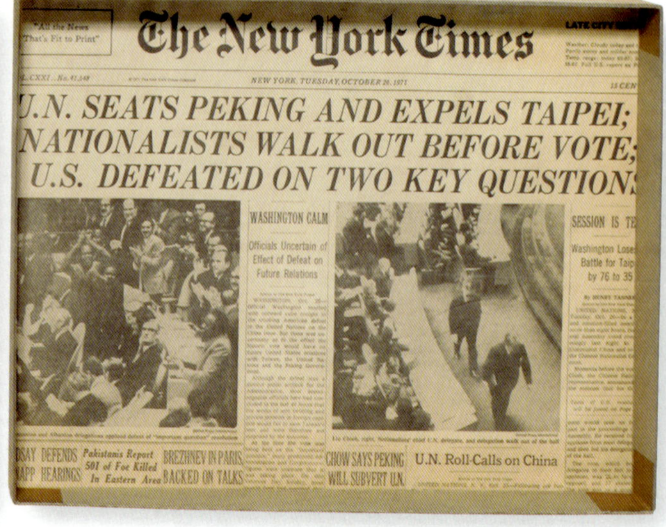
"All the News That's Fit to Print"

The New York Times

NEW YORK, TUESDAY, OCTOBER 26, 1971

U.N. SEATS PEKING AND EXPELS TAIPEI; NATIONALISTS WALK OUT BEFORE VOTE; U.S. DEFEATED ON TWO KEY QUESTIONS

WASHINGTON CALM

Officials Uncertain of Effect of Defeat on Future Relations

SESSION IS TE

Washington Loses Battle for Taip by 76 to 35

Pakistanis Report 501 of Foe Killed In Eastern Area

BREZHNEV IN PARIS, BACKED ON TALKS

CHOW SAYS PEKING WILL SUBVERT U.N.

U.N. Roll-Calls on China

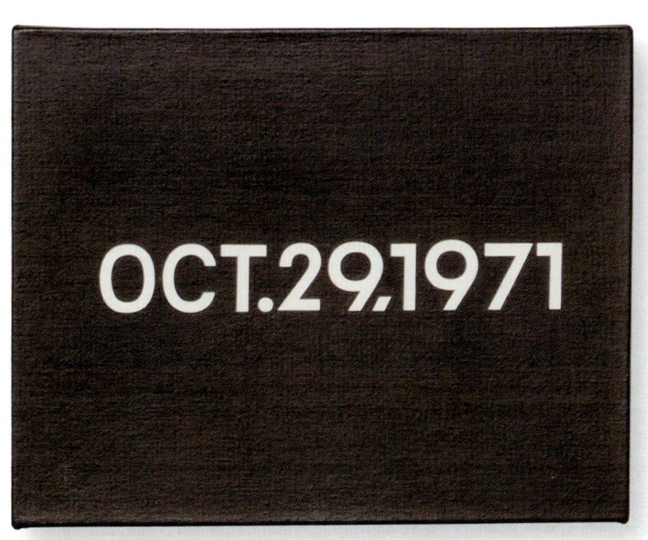
OCT.29,1971

OCT. 29, 1971

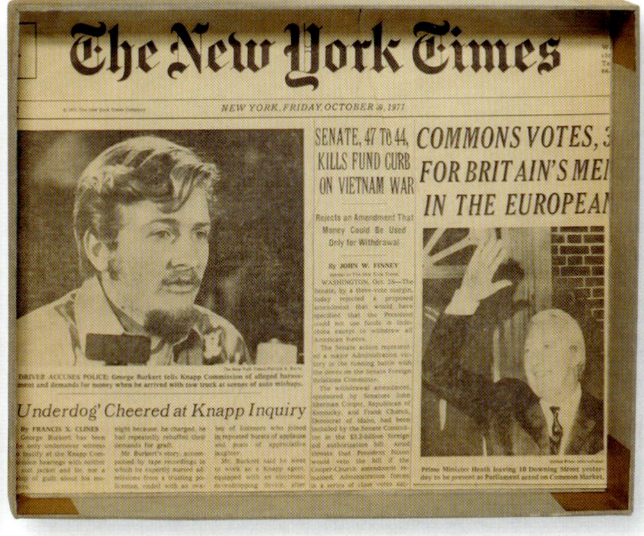
The New York Times
NEW YORK, FRIDAY, OCTOBER 29, 1971
SENATE, 47 TO 44, KILLS FUND CURB ON VIETNAM WAR
Rejects an Amendment That Money Could Be Used Only for Withdrawal
By JOHN W. FINNEY
COMMONS VOTES, 3
FOR BRITAIN'S ME
IN THE EUROPEAN
'Underdog' Cheered at Knapp Inquiry
By FRANCIS X. CLINES

On Kawara
Japanese, b. Kariya, 1933
One Million Years, 1970–71
Ink on paper, plastic sleeves,
and three-ring binders
Each 11⅝ × 9¼ × 3⅛ inches
Joseph H. Hirshhorn Purchase Fund, 2007
The Panza Collection (07.56)

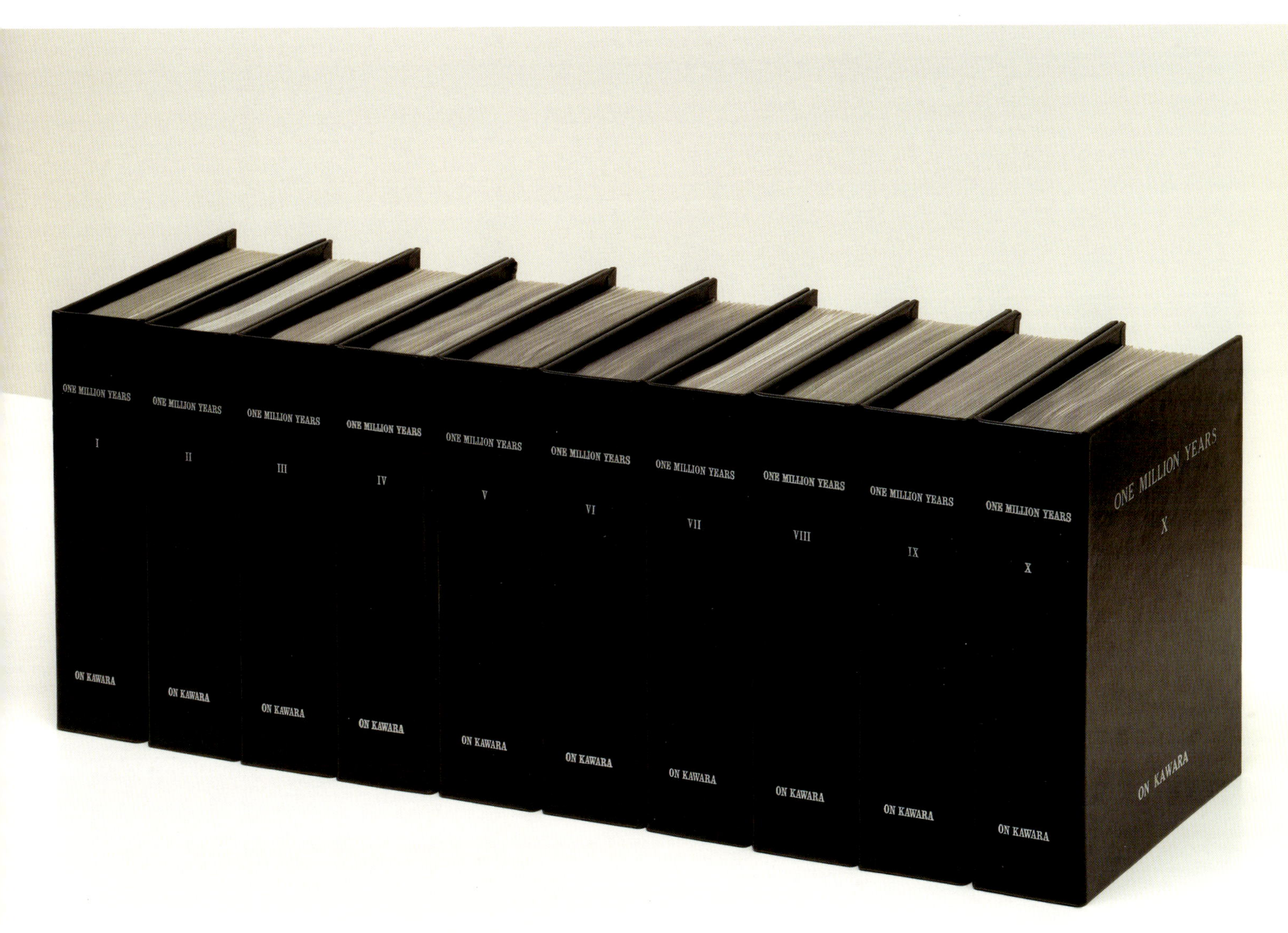
ONE MILLION YEARS
I
ON KAWARA
ONE MILLION YEARS
II
ON KAWARA
ONE MILLION YEARS
III
ON KAWARA
ONE MILLION YEARS
IV
ON KAWARA
ONE MILLION YEARS
V
ON KAWARA
ONE MILLION YEARS
VI
ON KAWARA
ONE MILLION YEARS
VII
ON KAWARA
ONE MILLION YEARS
VIII
ON KAWARA
ONE MILLION YEARS
IX
ON KAWARA
ONE MILLION YEARS
X
ON KAWARA
ONE MILLION YEARS
X
ON KAWARA

Roman Opalka
Polish, b. Abbeville, France, 1931
1965/1–∞: Detail 460260–484052,
Begun 1965
Acrylic paint on canvas
77 × 53¼ inches
Joseph H. Hirshhorn Purchase Fund, 2007
The Panza Collection (07.71)

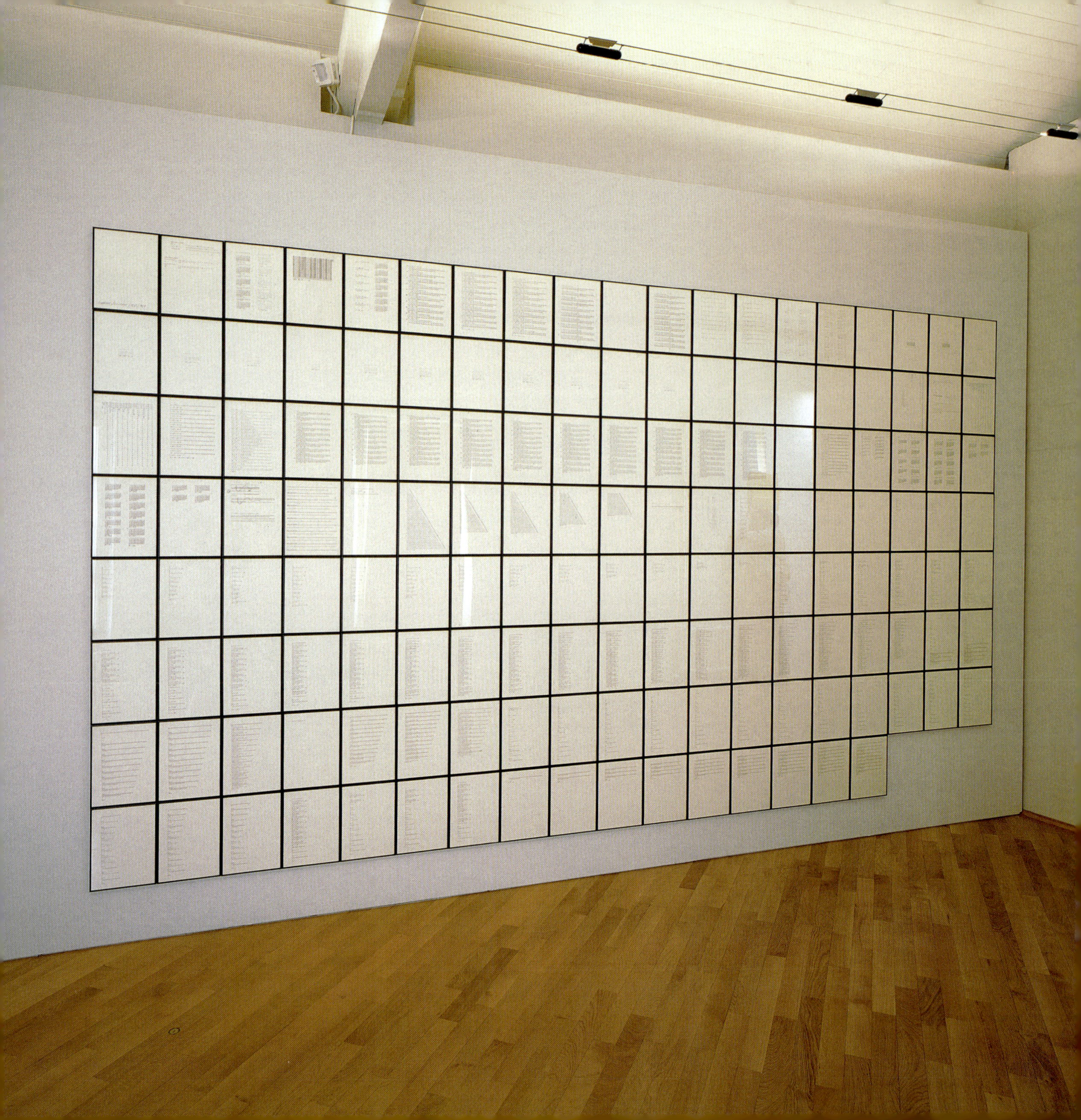

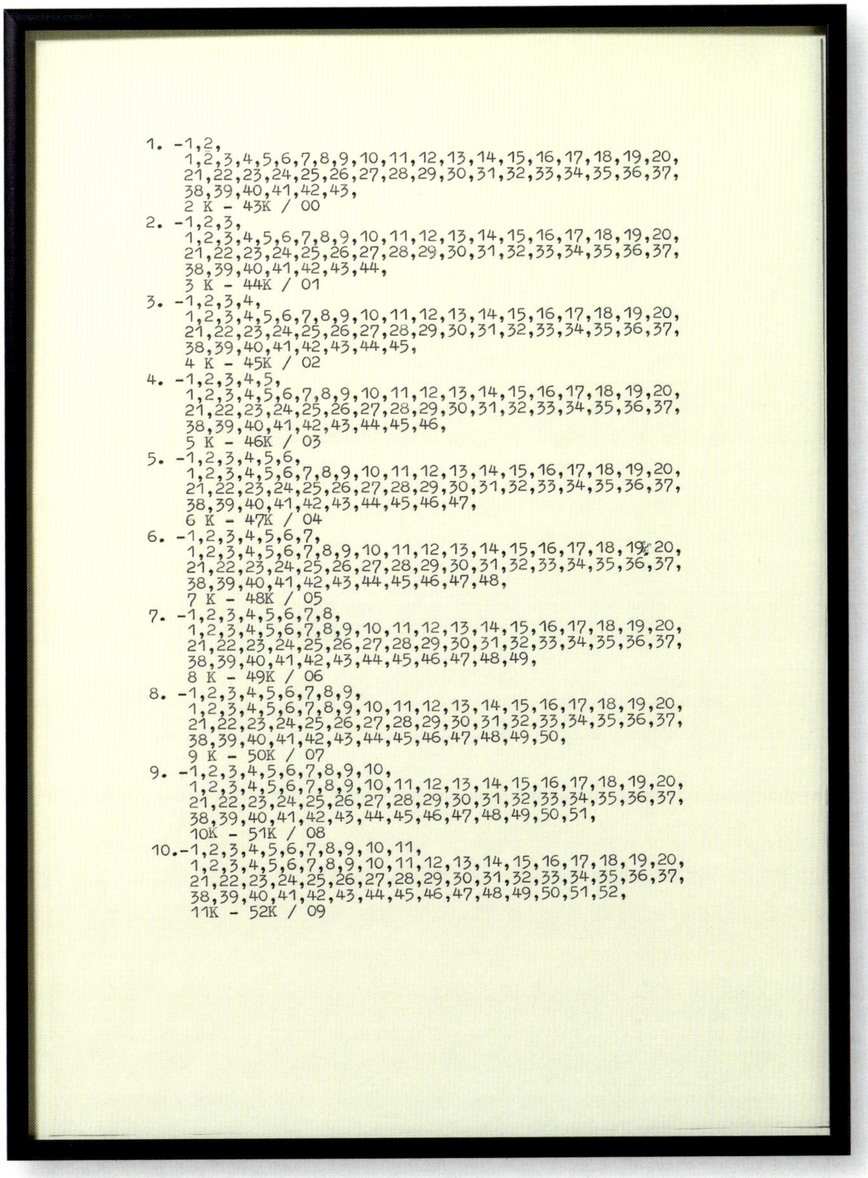

```
1. -1,2,
    1,2,3,4,5,6,7,8,9,10,11,12,13,14,15,16,17,18,19,20,
    21,22,23,24,25,26,27,28,29,30,31,32,33,34,35,36,37,
    38,39,40,41,42,43,
    2 K - 43K / 00
2. -1,2,3,
    1,2,3,4,5,6,7,8,9,10,11,12,13,14,15,16,17,18,19,20,
    21,22,23,24,25,26,27,28,29,30,31,32,33,34,35,36,37,
    38,39,40,41,42,43,44,
    3 K - 44K / 01
3. -1,2,3,4,
    1,2,3,4,5,6,7,8,9,10,11,12,13,14,15,16,17,18,19,20,
    21,22,23,24,25,26,27,28,29,30,31,32,33,34,35,36,37,
    38,39,40,41,42,43,44,45,
    4 K - 45K / 02
4. -1,2,3,4,5,
    1,2,3,4,5,6,7,8,9,10,11,12,13,14,15,16,17,18,19,20,
    21,22,23,24,25,26,27,28,29,30,31,32,33,34,35,36,37,
    38,39,40,41,42,43,44,45,46,
    5 K - 46K / 03
5. -1,2,3,4,5,6,
    1,2,3,4,5,6,7,8,9,10,11,12,13,14,15,16,17,18,19,20,
    21,22,23,24,25,26,27,28,29,30,31,32,33,34,35,36,37,
    38,39,40,41,42,43,44,45,46,47,
    6 K - 47K / 04
6. -1,2,3,4,5,6,7,
    1,2,3,4,5,6,7,8,9,10,11,12,13,14,15,16,17,18,19,20,
    21,22,23,24,25,26,27,28,29,30,31,32,33,34,35,36,37,
    38,39,40,41,42,43,44,45,46,47,48,
    7 K - 48K / 05
7. -1,2,3,4,5,6,7,8,
    1,2,3,4,5,6,7,8,9,10,11,12,13,14,15,16,17,18,19,20,
    21,22,23,24,25,26,27,28,29,30,31,32,33,34,35,36,37,
    38,39,40,41,42,43,44,45,46,47,48,49,
    8 K - 49K / 06
8. -1,2,3,4,5,6,7,8,9,
    1,2,3,4,5,6,7,8,9,10,11,12,13,14,15,16,17,18,19,20,
    21,22,23,24,25,26,27,28,29,30,31,32,33,34,35,36,37,
    38,39,40,41,42,43,44,45,46,47,48,49,50,
    9 K - 50K / 07
9. -1,2,3,4,5,6,7,8,9,10,
    1,2,3,4,5,6,7,8,9,10,11,12,13,14,15,16,17,18,19,20,
    21,22,23,24,25,26,27,28,29,30,31,32,33,34,35,36,37,
    38,39,40,41,42,43,44,45,46,47,48,49,50,51,
    10K - 51K / 08
10.-1,2,3,4,5,6,7,8,9,10,11,
    1,2,3,4,5,6,7,8,9,10,11,12,13,14,15,16,17,18,19,20,
    21,22,23,24,25,26,27,28,29,30,31,32,33,34,35,36,37,
    38,39,40,41,42,43,44,45,46,47,48,49,50,51,52,
    11K - 52K / 09
```

OPPOSITE

Hanne Darboven
German, b. Munich, 1941
27K-No8-No26, 1968–69
Typewriter ink and graphite on paper (149 sheets)
Each sheet 11⅝ × 8¼ inches
Joseph H. Hirshhorn Purchase Fund, 2007
The Panza Collection (07.41)

LEFT AND FOLLOWING PAGES

Details (sheets 41, 62, and 136)

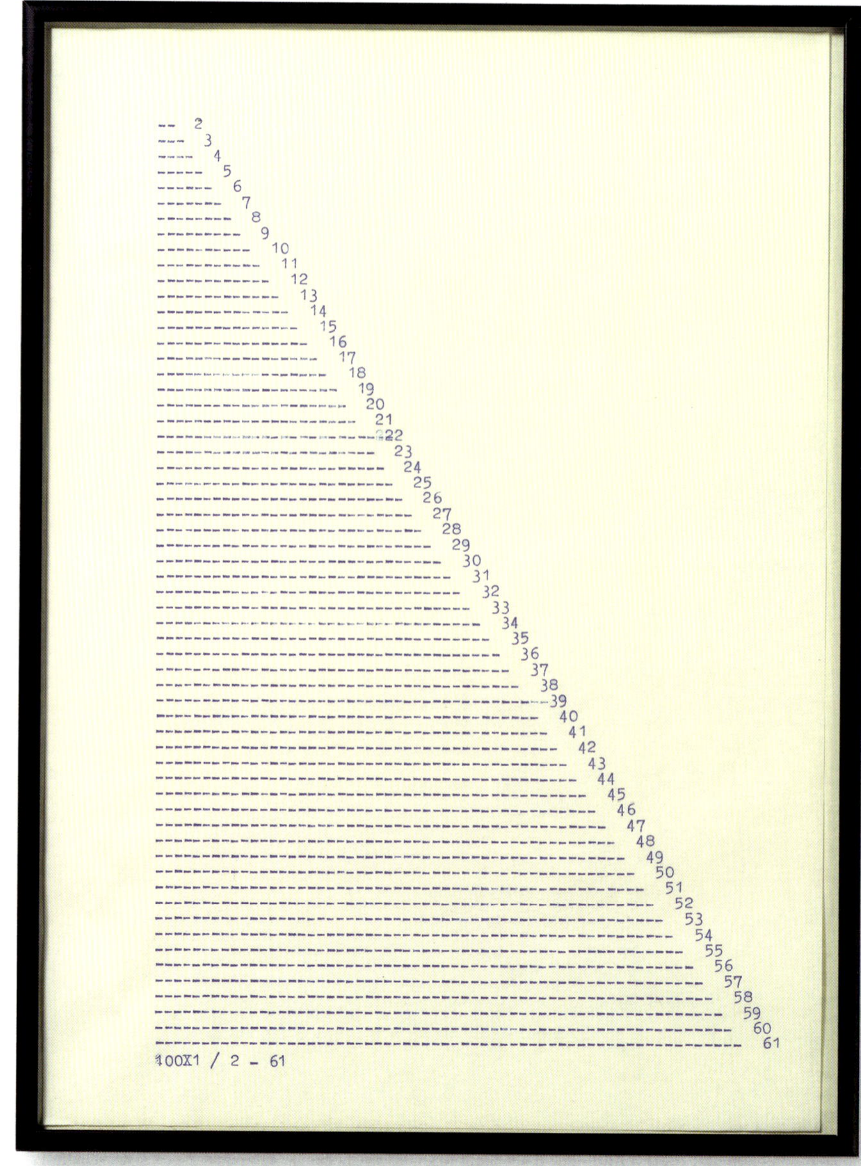
100X1 / 2 - 61

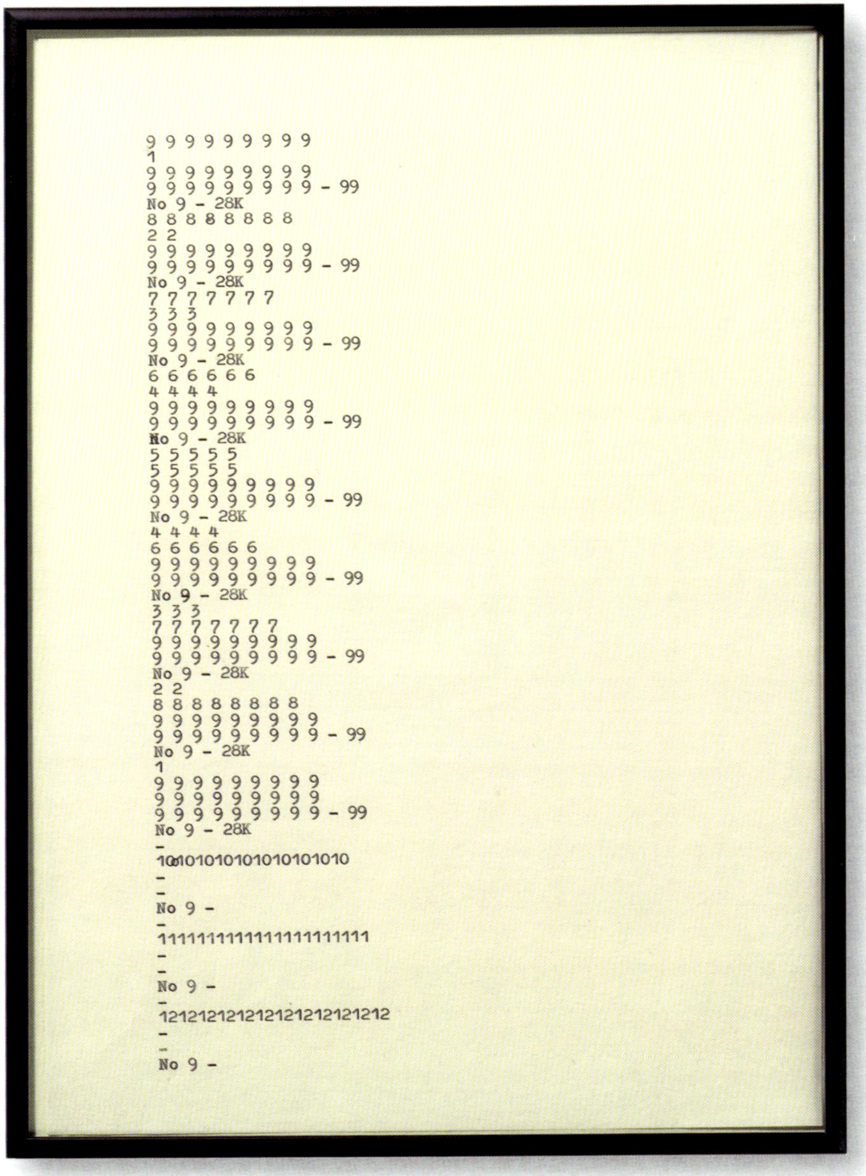

```
9 9 9 9 9 9 9 9 9
1
9 9 9 9 9 9 9 9 9
9 9 9 9 9 9 9 9 9 - 99
No 9 - 28K
8 8 8 8 8 8 8 8
2 2
9 9 9 9 9 9 9 9 9
9 9 9 9 9 9 9 9 9 - 99
No 9 - 28K
7 7 7 7 7 7 7
3 3 3
9 9 9 9 9 9 9 9 9
9 9 9 9 9 9 9 9 9 - 99
No 9 - 28K
6 6 6 6 6 6
4 4 4 4
9 9 9 9 9 9 9 9 9
9 9 9 9 9 9 9 9 9 - 99
No 9 - 28K
5 5 5 5 5
5 5 5 5 5
9 9 9 9 9 9 9 9 9
9 9 9 9 9 9 9 9 9 - 99
No 9 - 28K
4 4 4 4
6 6 6 6 6 6
9 9 9 9 9 9 9 9 9
9 9 9 9 9 9 9 9 9 - 99
No 9 - 28K
3 3 3
7 7 7 7 7 7 7
9 9 9 9 9 9 9 9 9
9 9 9 9 9 9 9 9 9 - 99
No 9 - 28K
2 2
8 8 8 8 8 8 8 8
9 9 9 9 9 9 9 9 9
9 9 9 9 9 9 9 9 9 - 99
No 9 - 28K
1
9 9 9 9 9 9 9 9 9
9 9 9 9 9 9 9 9 9
9 9 9 9 9 9 9 9 9 - 99
No 9 - 28K
-
10101010101010101010
-
-
No 9 -
-
1111111111111111111111
-
-
No 9 -
-
12121212121212121212121212
-
-
No 9 -
```

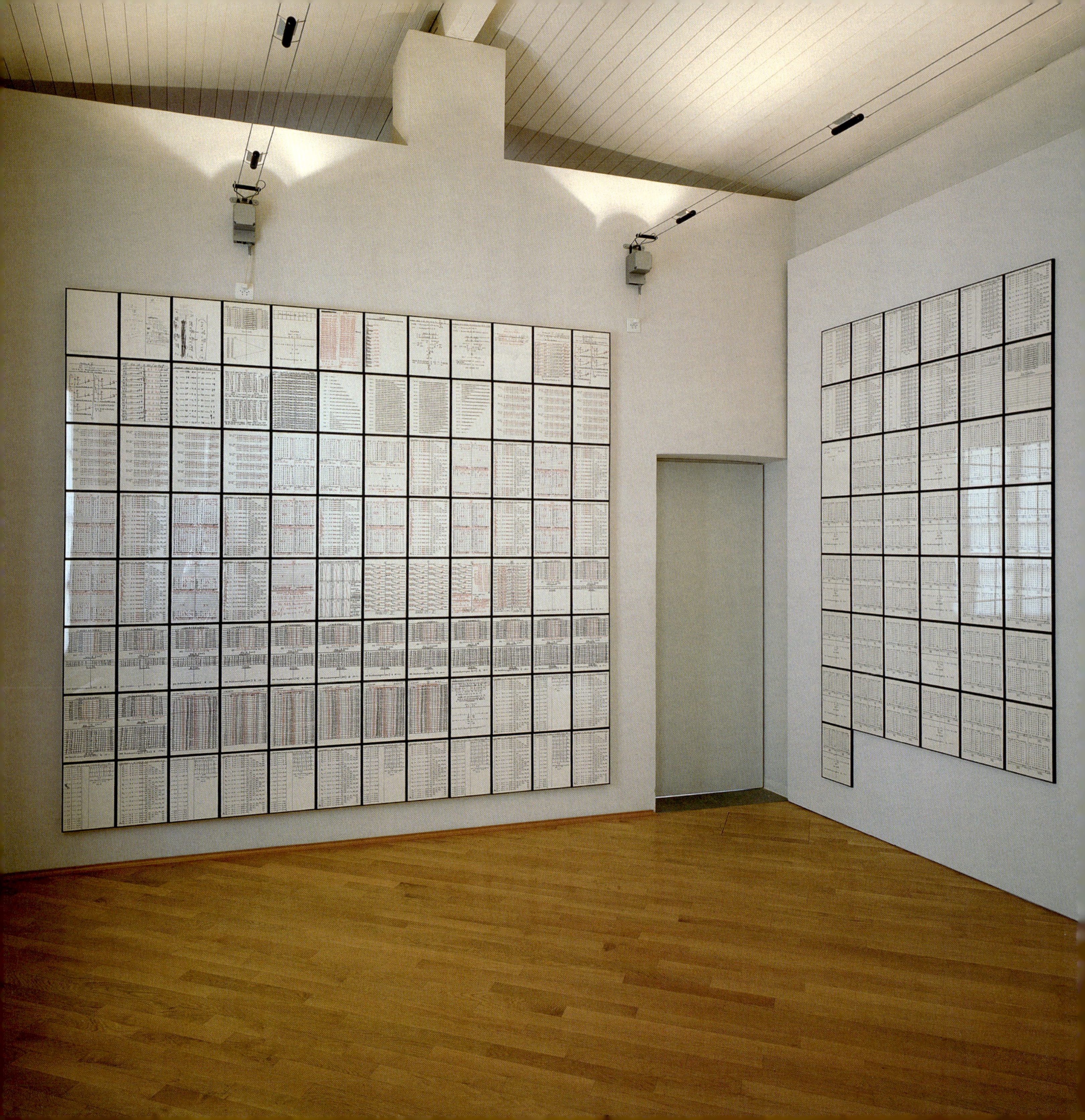

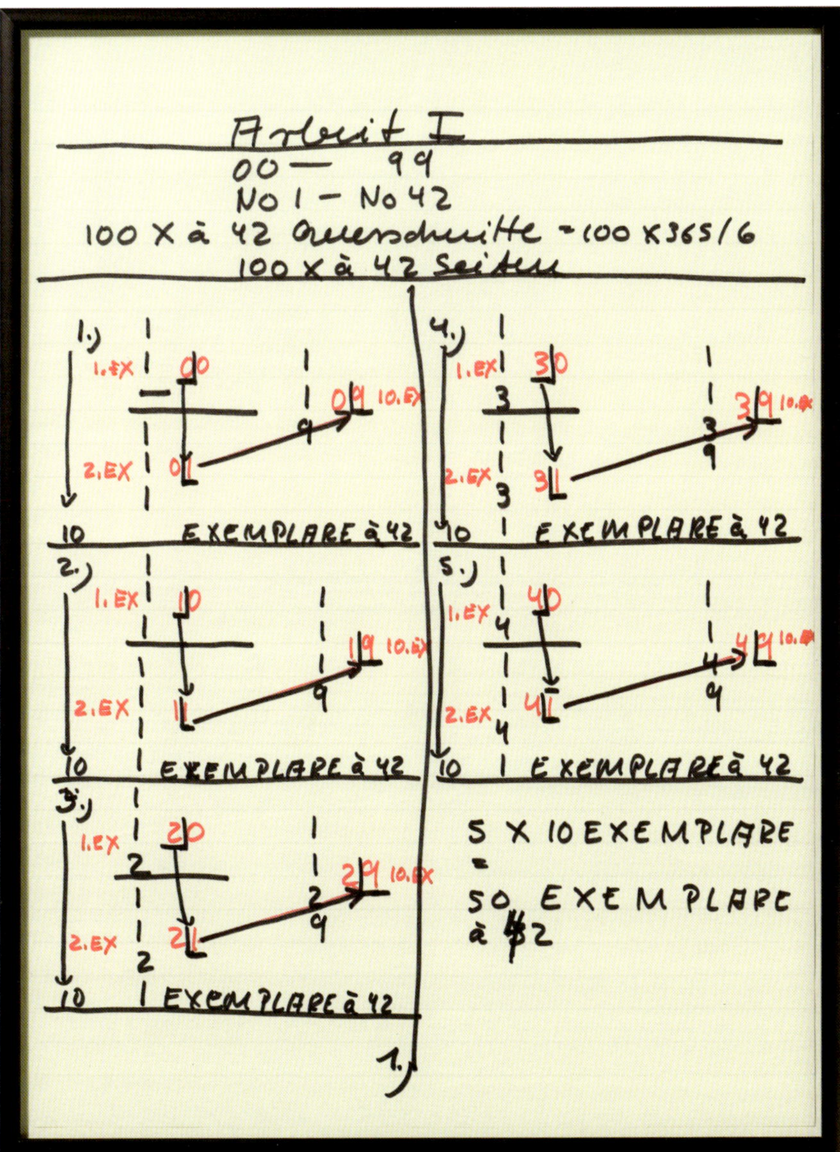

OPPOSITE
Hanne Darboven
German, b. Munich, 1941
00-99=No1-2K-20K, 1969–70
Ink, graphite, and lithographs on paper (140 sheets)
139 sheets 11⅝ × 8¼ inches;
1 sheet 7⅜ × 2¼
Joseph H. Hirshhorn Purchase Fund, 2007
The Panza Collection (07.42)

LEFT AND FOLLOWING PAGES
Details (sheets 12, 21, and 137)

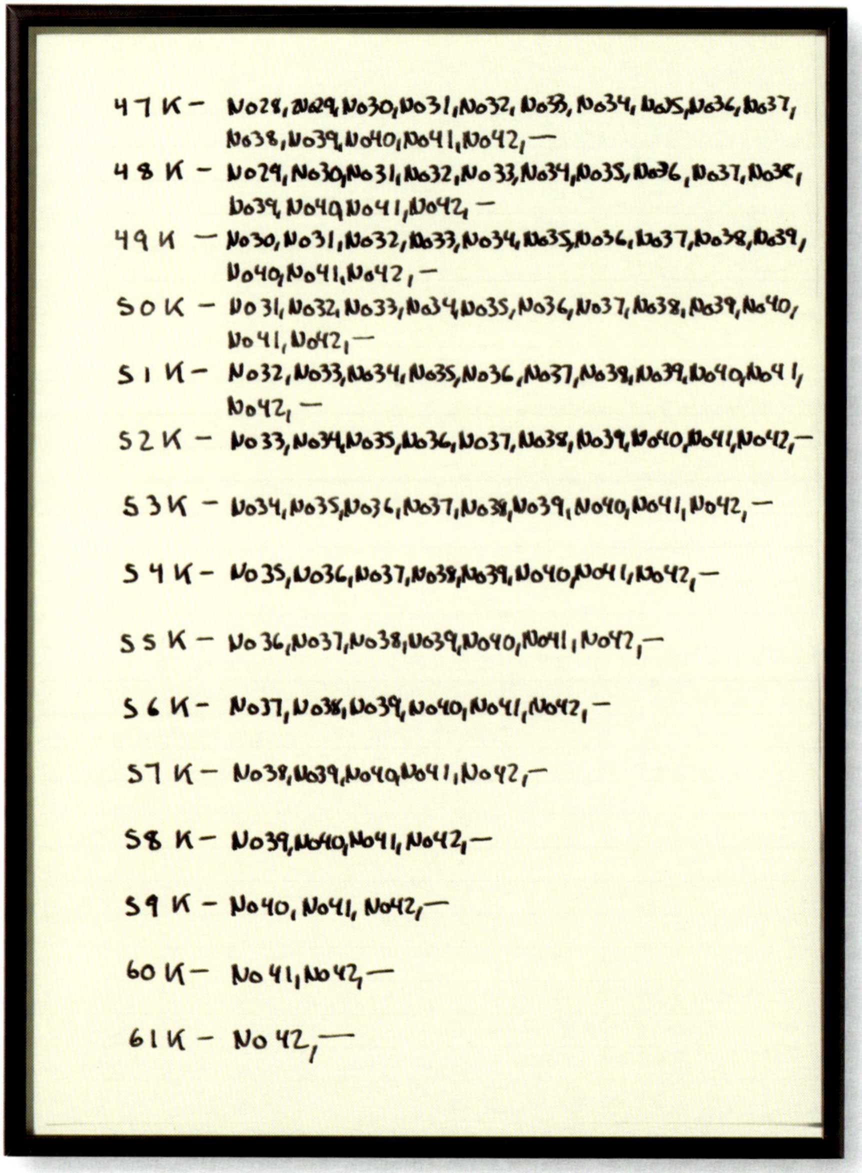

47 K – No28, No29, No30, No31, No32, No33, No34, No35, No36, No37,
No38, No39, No40, No41, No42, –
48 K – No29, No30, No31, No32, No33, No34, No35, No36, No37, No38,
No39, No40, No41, No42, –
49 K – No30, No31, No32, No33, No34, No35, No36, No37, No38, No39,
No40, No41, No42, –
50 K – No31, No32, No33, No34, No35, No36, No37, No38, No39, No40,
No41, No42, –
51 K – No32, No33, No34, No35, No36, No37, No38, No39, No40, No41,
No42, –
52 K – No33, No34, No35, No36, No37, No38, No39, No40, No41, No42, –

53 K – No34, No35, No36, No37, No38, No39, No40, No41, No42, –

54 K – No35, No36, No37, No38, No39, No40, No41, No42, –

55 K – No36, No37, No38, No39, No40, No41, No42, –

56 K – No37, No38, No39, No40, No41, No42, –

57 K – No38, No39, No40, No41, No42, –

58 K – No39, No40, No41, No42, –

59 K – No40, No41, No42, –

60 K – No41, No42, –

61 K – No42, –

No 10 = 11K → 20K
10 + 1 + 0 + 0 — 11
" " " " 0 + 1 —
" " " " 0 + 2 —
" " " " 0 + 3 —
" " " " 0 + 4 —
" " " " 0 + 5 —
" " " " 0 + 6 —
" " " " 0 + 7 —
" " " " 0 + 8 —
" " " " 0 + 9 — 20
10 zeichnungen
00 → 09
I

No 10 = 12K → 21K
10 + 1 + 1 + 0 — 12
" " " " 1 + 1 —
" " " " 1 + 2 —
" " " " 1 + 3 —
" " " " 1 + 4 —
" " " " 1 + 5 —
" " " " 1 + 6 —
" " " " 1 + 7 —
" " " " 1 + 8 —
" " " " 1 + 9 — 21
10 zeichnungen
10 → 19
II

No 10 = 13K → 22K
10 + 1 + 2 + 0 — 13
" " " " 2 + 1 —
" " " " 2 + 2 —
" " " " 2 + 3 —
" " " " 2 + 4 —
" " " " 2 + 5 —
" " " " 2 + 6 —
" " " " 2 + 7 —
" " " " 2 + 8 —
" " " " 2 + 9 — 22
10 zeichnungen
20 → 29
III

No 10 = 14K → 23K
10 + 1 + 3 + 0 — 14
" " " " 3 + 1 —
" " " " 3 + 2 —
" " " " 3 + 3 —
" " " " 3 + 4 —
" " " " 3 + 5 —
" " " " 3 + 6 —
" " " " 3 + 7 —
" " " " 3 + 8 —
" " " " 3 + 9 — 23
10 zeichnungen
30 → 39
IV

Richard Long, Hamish Fulton, Jan Dibbets

Richard Long
British, b. Bristol, England, 1945
Carrara Line, 1985
Marble
563 × 53⅛ inches
Joseph H. Hirshhorn Purchase Fund, 2007
The Panza Collection (07.66)

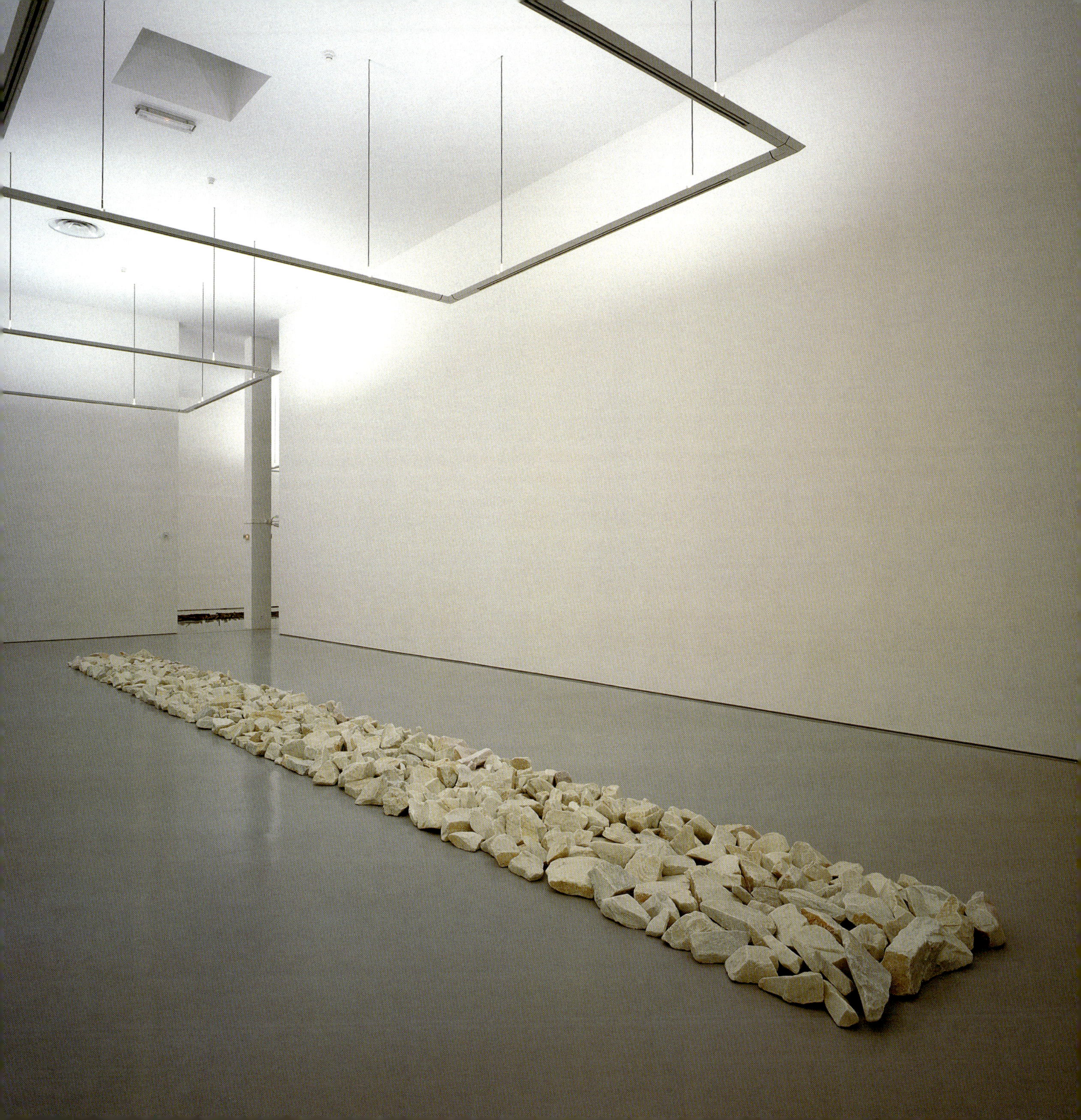

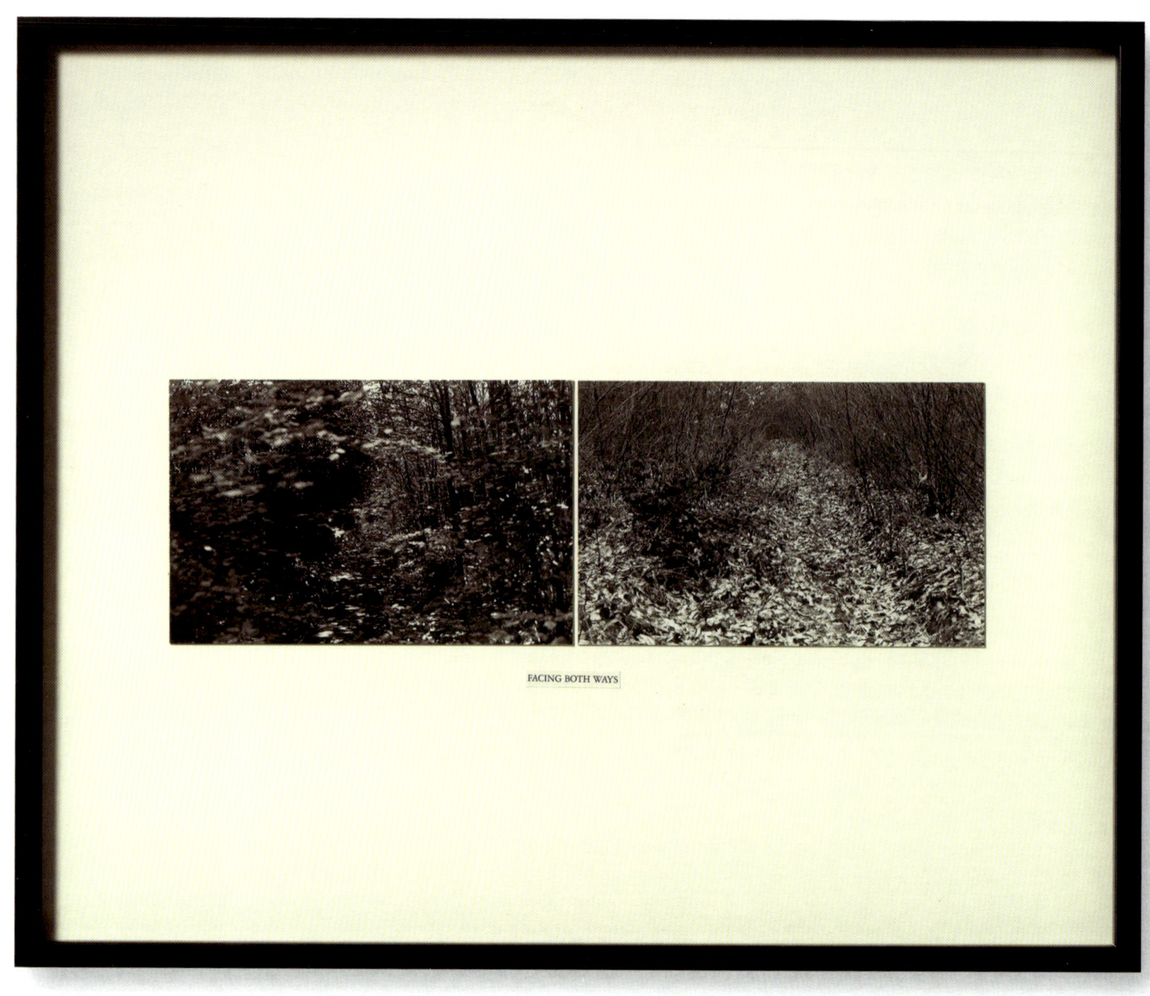

Hamish Fulton
British, b. London, England, 1946
Facing Both Ways, 1972
Gelatin silver prints and ink on paperboard
19⅞ × 23⅞ inches
Joseph H. Hirshhorn Purchase Fund, 2007
The Panza Collection (07.45)

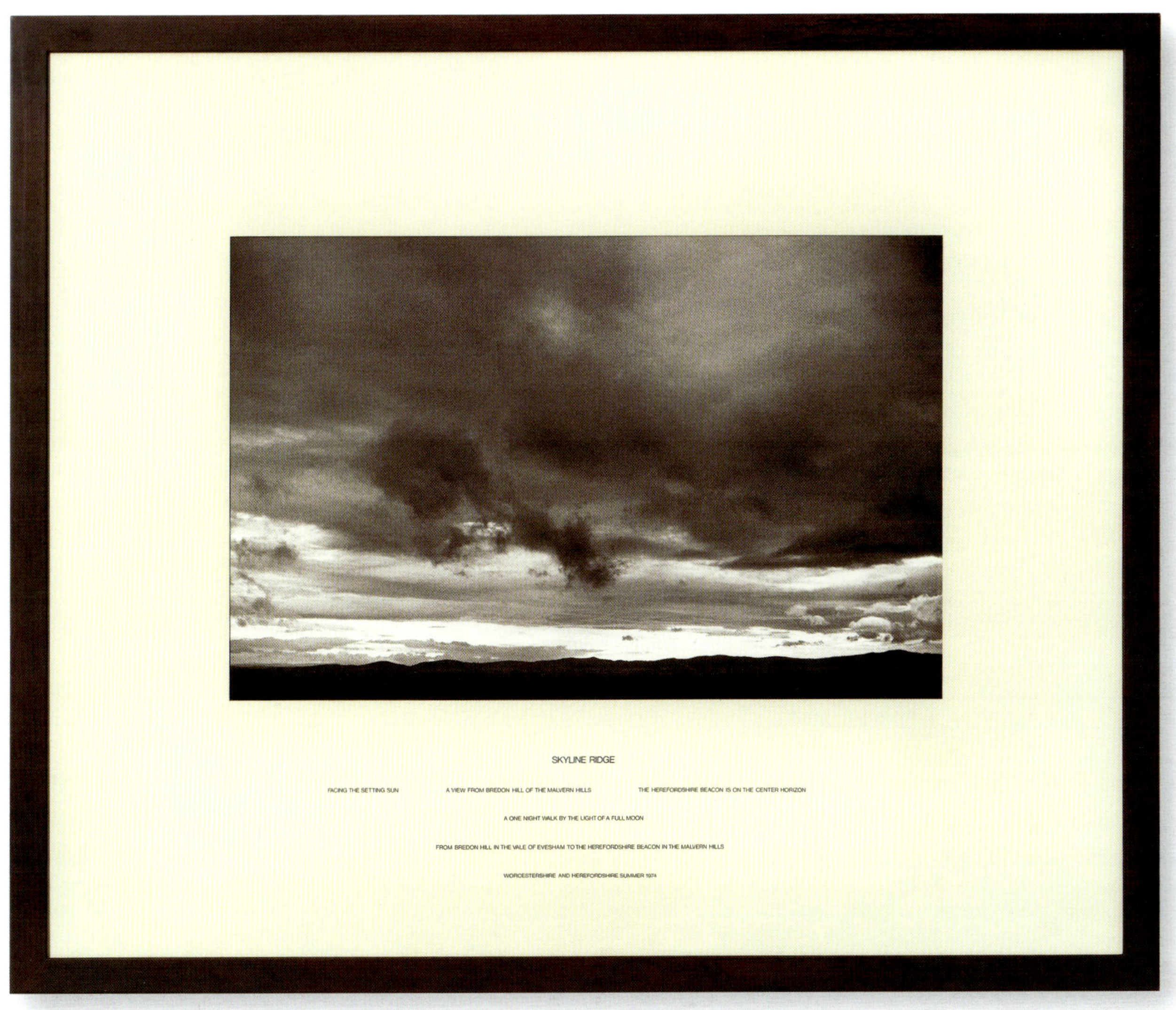

Hamish Fulton
British, b. London, England, 1946
Skyline Ridge, 1974
Gelatin silver print and ink on paperboard
38½ × 45½ inches
Joseph H. Hirshhorn Purchase Fund, 2007
The Panza Collection (07.46)

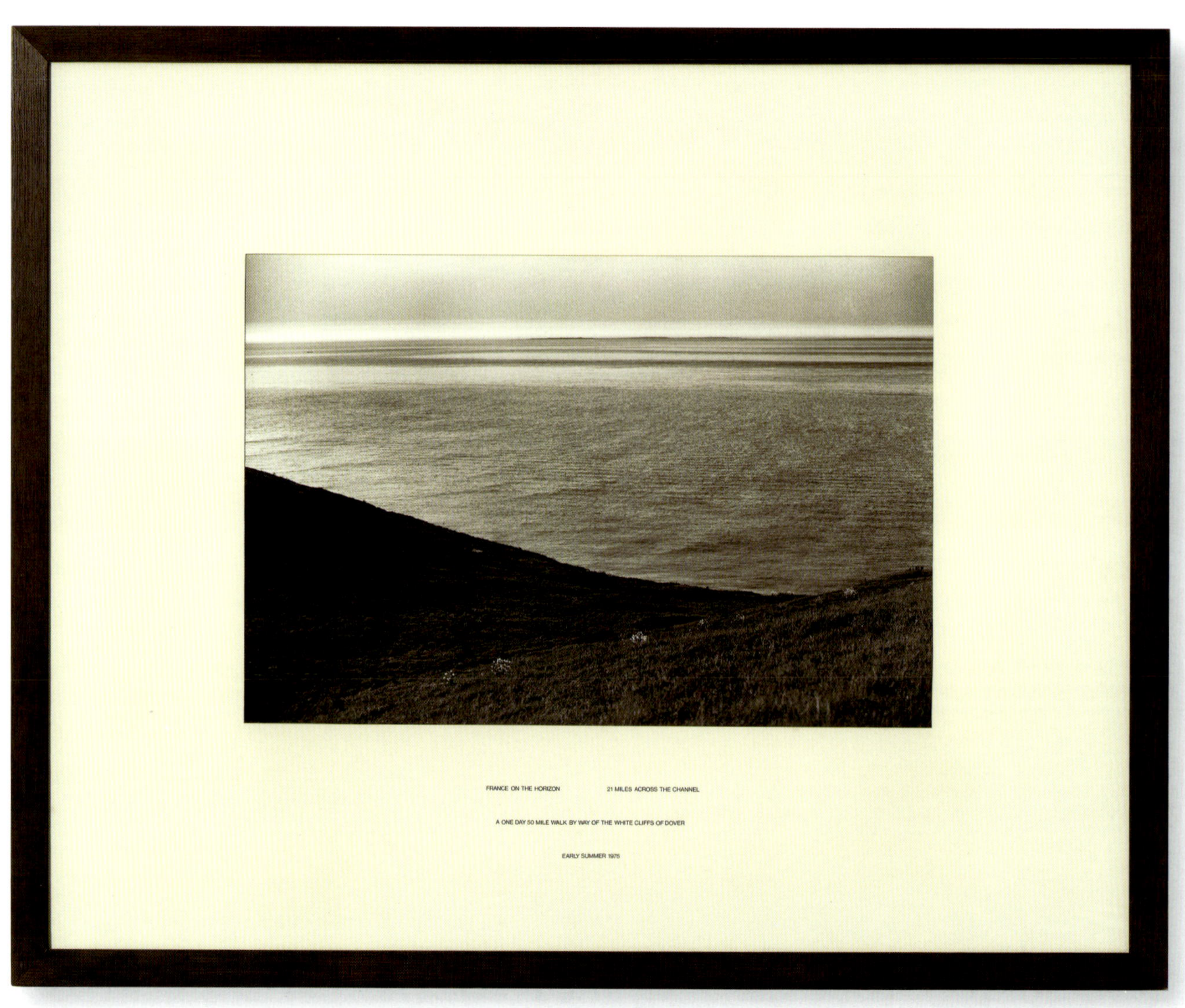

Hamish Fulton
British, b. London, England, 1946
France on the Horizon, 1975
Gelatin silver print and ink on paperboard
37 × 44⅞ inches
Joseph H. Hirshhorn Purchase Fund, 2007
The Panza Collection (07.47)

Hamish Fulton
British, b. London, England, 1946
Untitled – (Iceland 1975), 1975
Gelatin silver prints and ink on paperboard
39⅜ × 105⅝ × 1½ inches
Joseph H. Hirshhorn Purchase Fund, 2007
The Panza Collection (07.48)

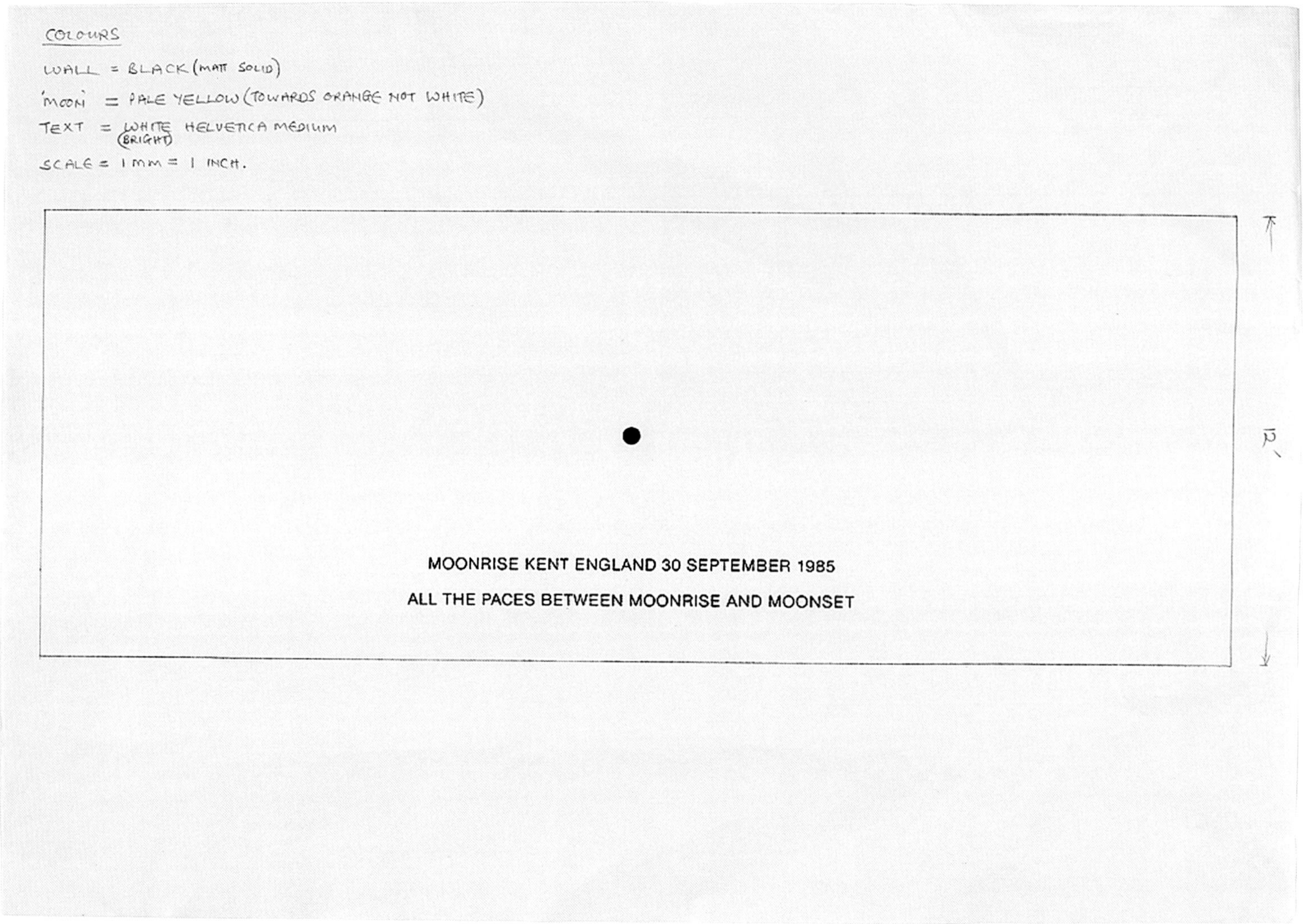

COLOURS

WALL = BLACK (MATT SOLID)

'MOON' = PALE YELLOW (TOWARDS ORANGE NOT WHITE)

TEXT = WHITE (BRIGHT) HELVETICA MEDIUM

SCALE = 1 MM = 1 INCH.

MOONRISE KENT ENGLAND 30 SEPTEMBER 1985

ALL THE PACES BETWEEN MOONRISE AND MOONSET

Hamish Fulton
British, b. London, England, 1946
Sketch and instructions for
Moonrise Kent England 30 September 1985, 1985
Paint and vinyl lettering on wall
144 × 384 inches
Joseph H. Hirshhorn Purchase Fund, 2007
The Panza Collection (07.49)

RIGHT

Jan Dibbets

Dutch, b. Weert, The Netherlands, 1941
Installation view at Guggenheim Bilbao Museoa of *The Shortest Day of 1970 Photographed in My House Every 6 Minutes from Sunrise til Sunset,* 1970
Gelatin silver prints on paper on aluminum
Each panel 4¾ × 55⅞ inches;
4¾ × 558¾ inches overall
Joseph H. Hirshhorn Purchase Fund, 2007
The Panza Collection (07.44)

BELOW

Details

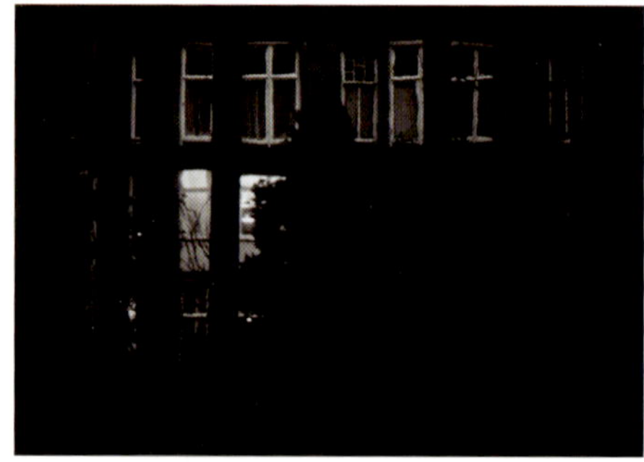

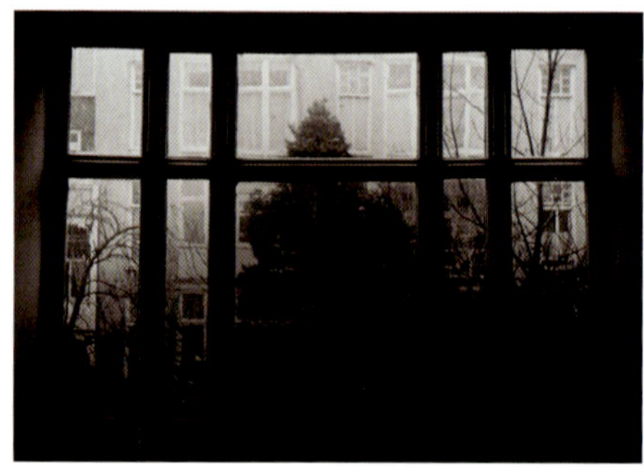

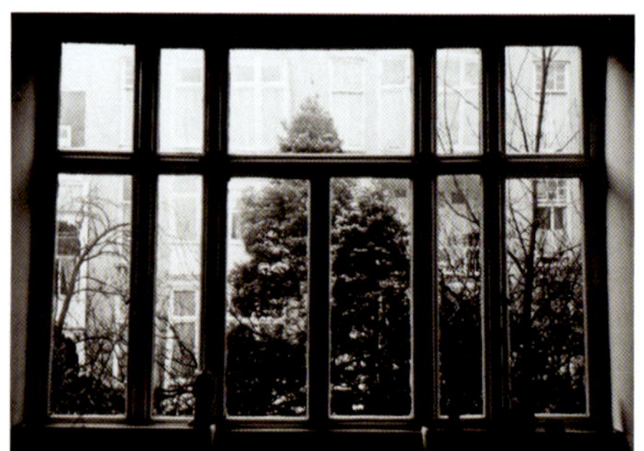

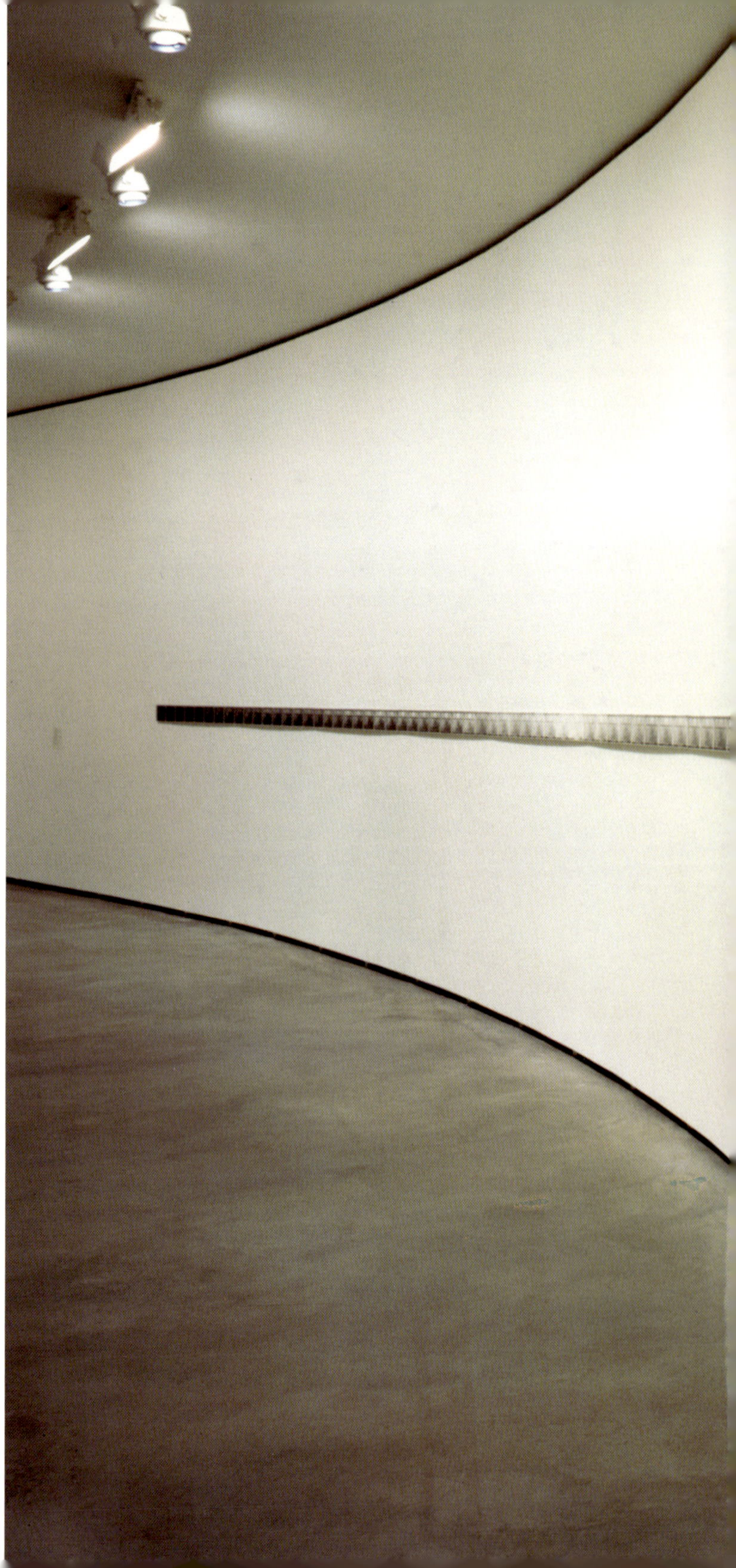

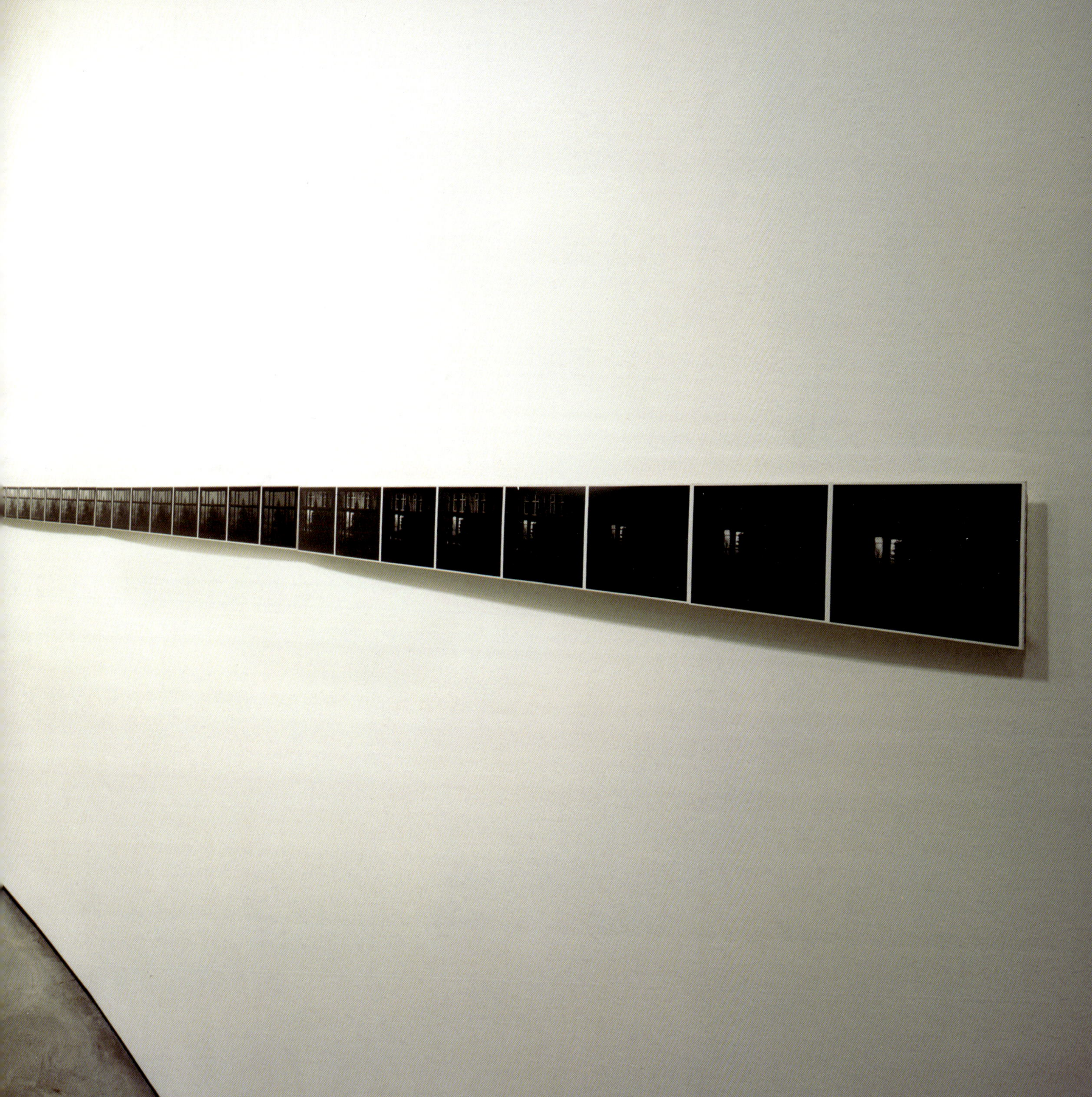

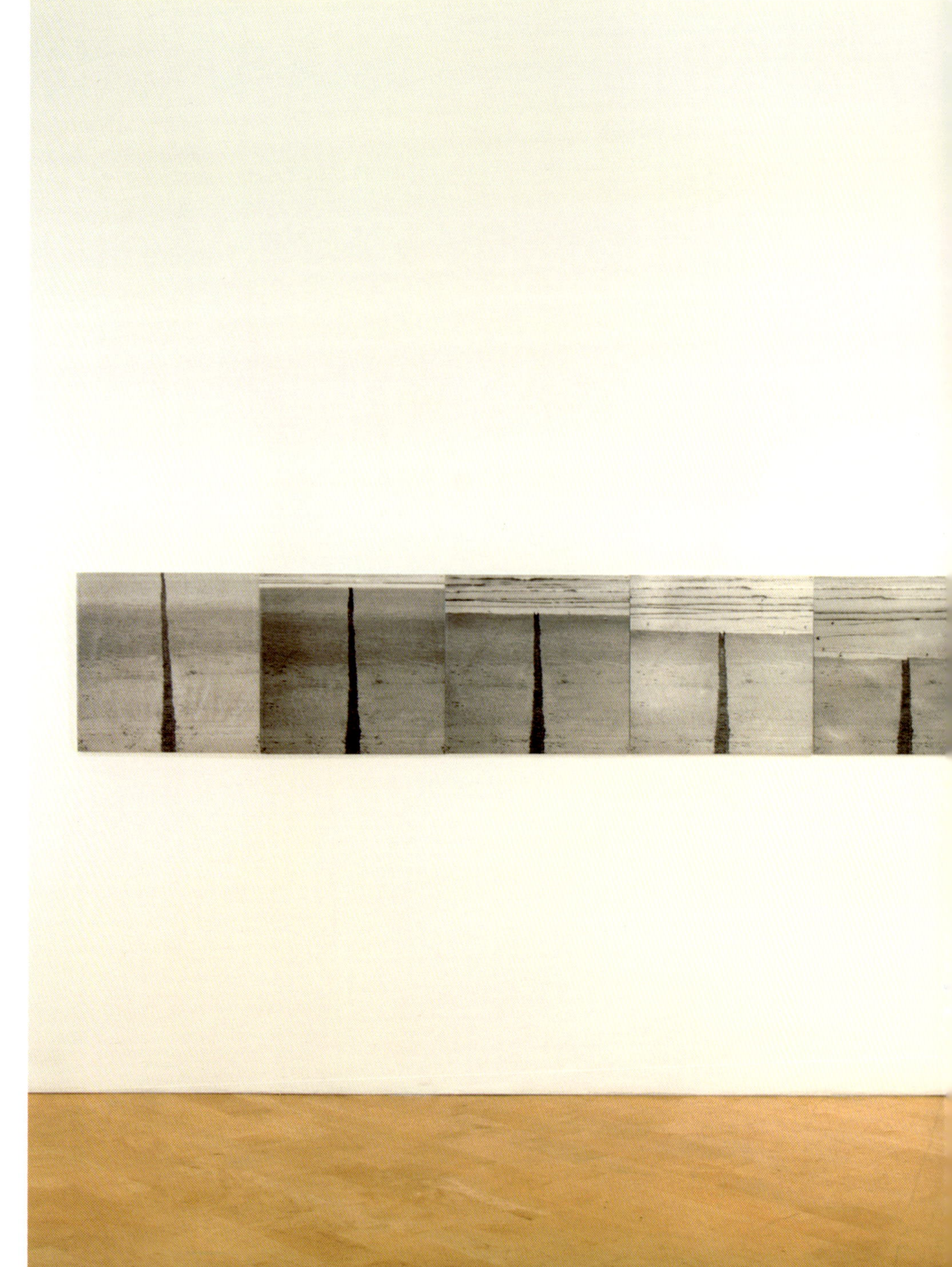

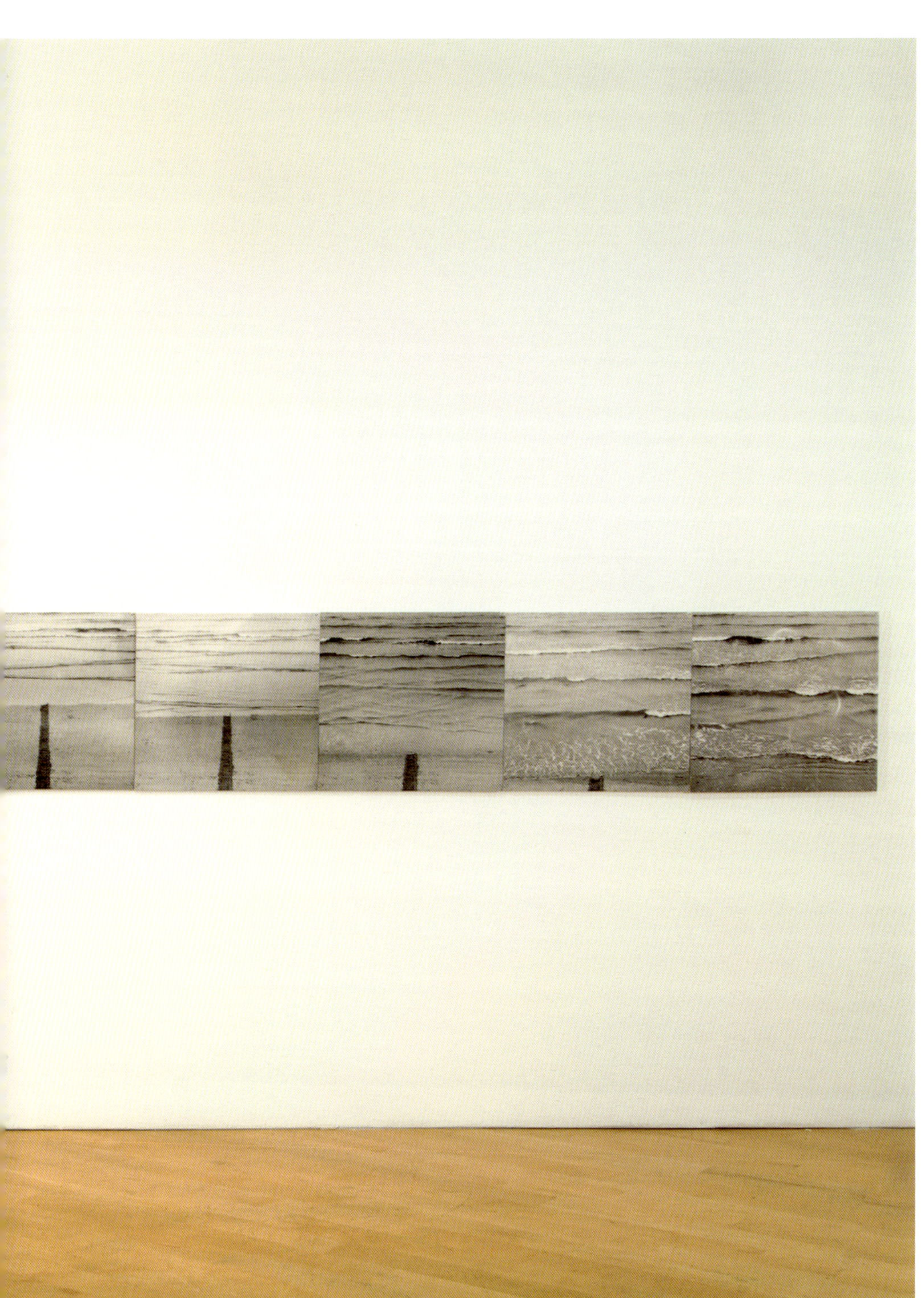

Jan Dibbets
Dutch, b. Weert, The Netherlands, 1941
Flood Tide, 1969
Gelatin silver prints
Overall 23¾ × 237⅛ inches
Joseph H. Hirshhorn Purchase Fund, 2007
The Panza Collection (07.43)

Bruce Nauman

Bruce Nauman
American, b. Fort Wayne, Indiana, 1941
Art Make-Up #1–4, 1967–68
16mm film transferred to DVD
Color. Sound
8–10 minutes each, approximately
Joseph H. Hirshhorn Purchase Fund, 2007
The Panza Collection (07.67)

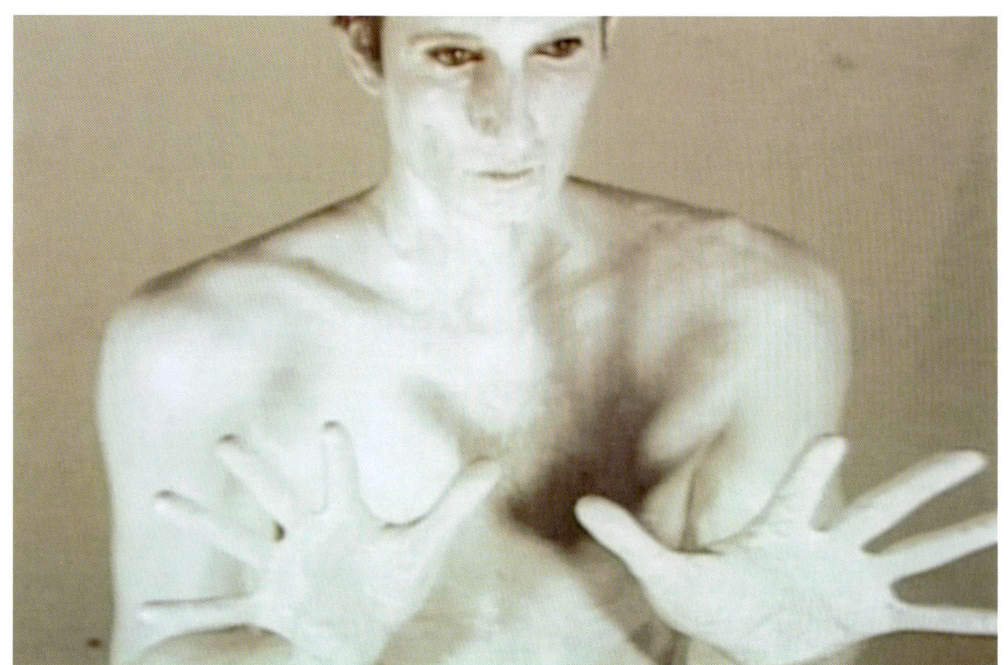

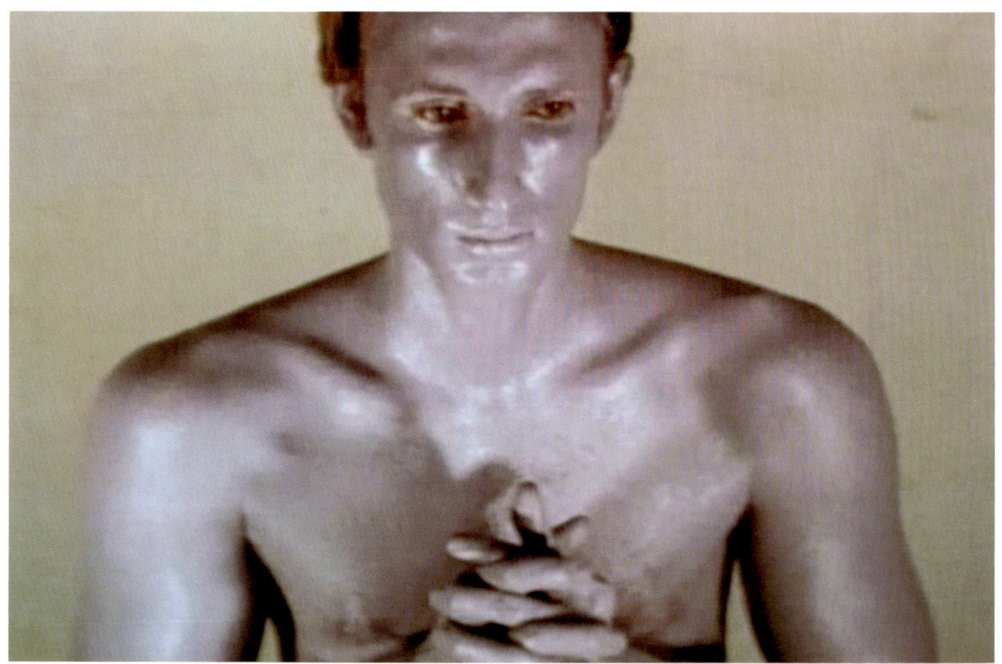

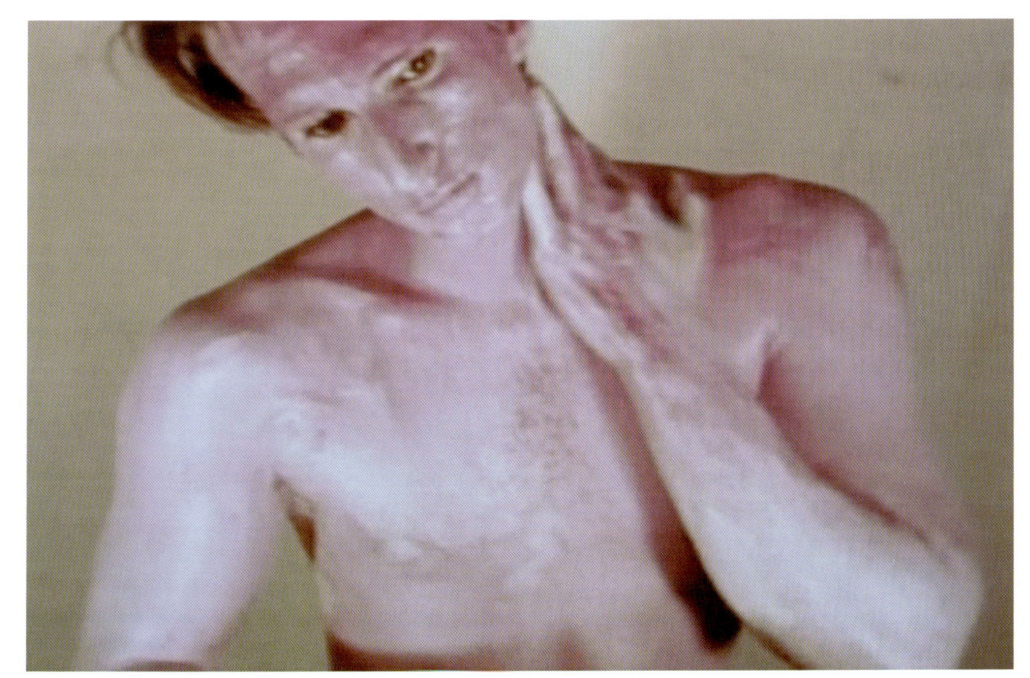

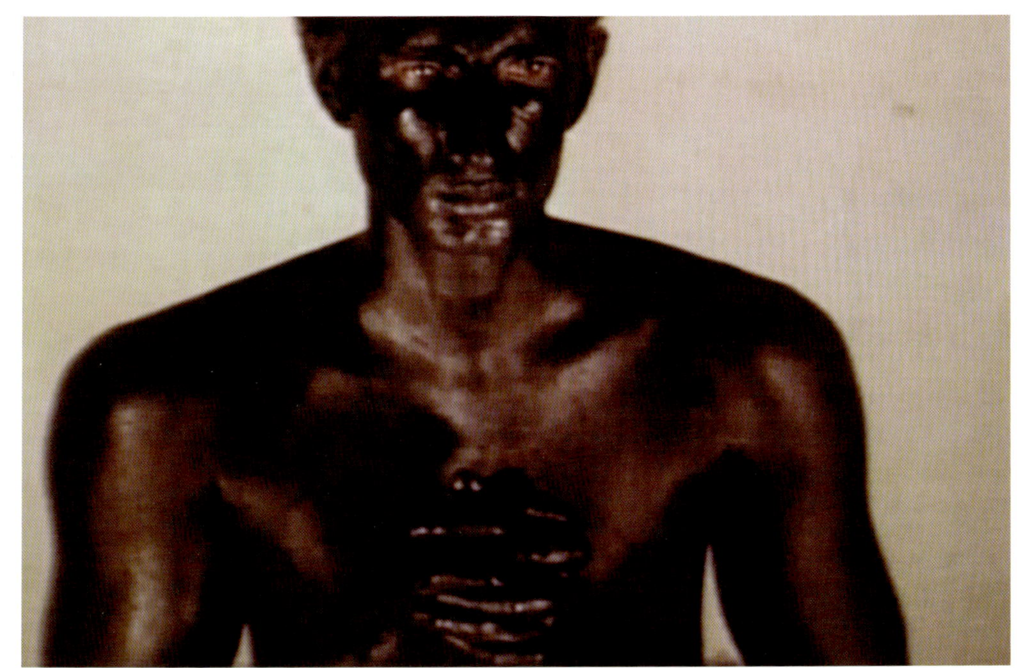

Photography Credits

We would like to thank all those who gave their kind permission to reproduce material. All reasonable efforts have been made to obtain copyright permission for the images in this book. The publishers apologize for any inadvertent errors or omissions.

Photographs © Giorgio Colombo, Milan, Italy: 10, 13, 14, 15, 20, 24/25, 42, 65, 74, 78, 83

Photographs by A. Zambianchi – Simply.it: cover, 36, 37, 38, 47, 50, 52, 58 (top), 59, 62, 63, 64

Photographs by Lee Stalsworth, Hirshhorn Museum and Sculpture Garden: frontispiece, 6, 22, 23, 26, 27, 28, 29, 30, 32, 39, 40, 41, 43, 44, 45, 46, 48, 49, 51, 53, 55, 56, 58 (bottom), 60, 61, 67, 68, 69, 71, 72, 75, 76, 77, 79, 80, 81, 84, 85, 86, 89, 90 (details), 92/93, 94/95

Photograph by Ugo Mulas: 19

Photograph by Seth Siegelaub: 21

Photograph by Dorothee Fischer: 57

©FMGB Guggenheim Bilbao Museoa, Photo Erika Ede, 2008. All rights reserved. Total or partial reproduction is prohibited: 90/91

© 2008 Jan Dibbets/Artists Rights Society (ARS), New York: title page, 90/91, 92/93

© 2008 Stephen Flavin/Artists Rights Society (ARS), New York: 16

© 2008 Estate of Douglas Huebler/Artists Rights Society (ARS), New York: 50, 51, 52, 53, 55

© 2008 Robert Irwin/Artists Rights Society (ARS), New York: 14, 26, 60, 61, 62, 63

© 2008 Franz Kline/Artists Rights Society (ARS), New York: 17

© 2008 Joseph Kosuth/Artists Rights Society (ARS), New York: 22, 36, 37, 38, 39, 40, 41

© 2008 Estate of Sol LeWitt/Artists Rights Society (ARS), New York: 24/25, 56, 57

© 2008 Bruce Nauman/Artists Rights Society (ARS), New York: 32, 94/95

© 2008 Roman Opalka/Artist Rights Society (ARS), New York/ADAGP, Paris: 6, 29, 72

© 2008 Lawrence Weiner/Artists Rights Society (ARS), New York: 23, 42, 43

© 2008 Doug Wheeler/Licensed by VAGA, New York, NY: 64